Celtic Tree Alphabets

"Another well-researched and capably written volume from Nigel Pennick's busy pen, *Celtic Tree Alphabets* does a fine job of communicating the history and lore of the Irish Ogham and Welsh Coelbren scripts. Highly recommended to anyone interested in Celtic traditions."

JOHN MICHAEL GREER, AUTHOR OF
*COELBREN: TRADITIONS, DIVINATION LORE, AND
MAGIC OF THE WELSH BARDIC ALPHABET*
AND *THE TWILIGHT OF PLUTO*

"Nigel Pennick's latest study of the history and symbolic meaning of the Irish Ogham alphabet and the Welsh Coelbren is the result of years of research and spiritual practice. The elemental powers of the associated trees, birds, and colors described by the author establish connections between the inner world of the soul and the forces of nature. This work on Celtic spirituality has the potential to open many doors for the reader."

PATRICK MCFADZEAN, AUTHOR OF
VASTU VIDYA: STUDIES IN INDIAN GEOMANCY

"This book is a treasure trove of detail on Celtic scripts sourced directly from original texts. Systematically presented, it is enriched with tales of folklore practices and archival discoveries that debunk popular myths. Beautifully illustrated with original artwork by the author."

PRUDENCE JONES, COAUTHOR OF
A HISTORY OF PAGAN EUROPE

"*Celtic Tree Alphabets* delves into the Ogham through a fascinating exploration of Irish history and mythology, drawing from authentic historical texts. Nigel Pennick skillfully navigates the origins of the Ogham, delving into the deities of the sacred forest, Celtic tree lore, and Welsh Bardic scripts. Additionally, he examines Coelbren, the Welsh 'Bardic alphabet' attributed to Bard Iolo Morganwg. In his latest work, Pennick makes complex knowledge accessible and engaging, offering readers a wealth of information to explore."

JUNE KENT, EDITOR OF
INDIE SHAMAN MAGAZINE

Celtic Tree Alphabets

Mystic Signs and Symbols of **Ogham** and **Coelbren**

Nigel Pennick

Destiny Books

Rochester, Vermont

Destiny Books
One Park Street
Rochester, Vermont 05767
www.DestinyBooks.com

SUSTAINABLE FORESTRY INITIATIVE
Certified Sourcing
www.forests.org
SFI-00854

Text stock is SFI certified

Destiny Books is a division of Inner Traditions International

Cataloging-in-Publication Data for this title is available from the Library of Congress

ISBN 978-1-64411-748-4 (print)
ISBN 978-1-64411-749-1 (ebook)

Printed and bound in the United States by Lake Book Manufacturing, LLC
The text stock is SFI certified. The Sustainable Forestry Initiative® program promotes
sustainable forest management.

10 9 8 7 6 5 4 3 2 1

Text design and layout by Kenleigh Manseau
This book was typeset in Garamond Premier Pro with Dutch Mediaeval Pro and
Parisine Plus Std used as display typefaces.

To send correspondence to the author of this book, mail a first-class letter to the
author c/o Inner Traditions • Bear & Company, One Park Street, Rochester, VT
05767, and we will forward the communication.

Scan the QR code and save 25% at InnerTraditions.com.
Browse over 2,000 titles on spirituality, the occult, ancient
mysteries, new science, holistic health, and natural medicine.

Midir, guardian of the gateway to the Otherworld. The Bardo-Druidic
alphabets are inner gateways to the same realms.

Contents

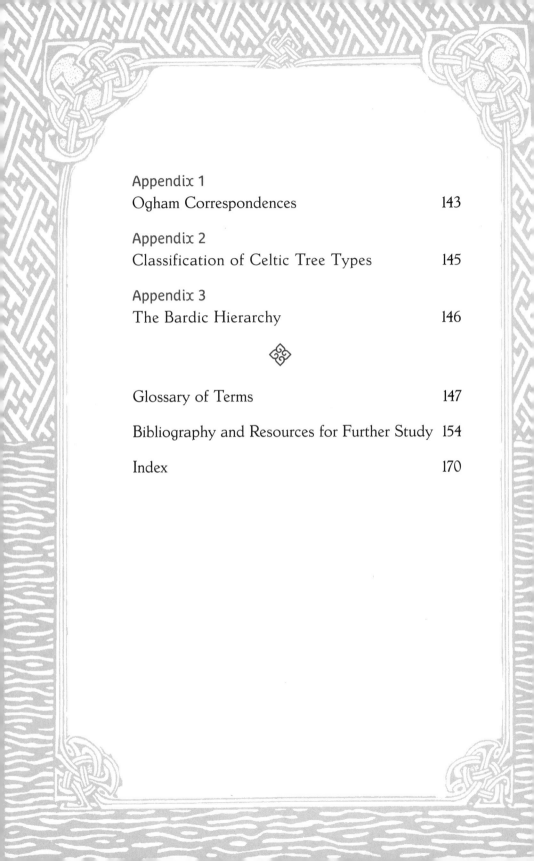

Acknowledgments

I wish to thank the following people and institutions for various assistance or information that was forthcoming at certain times in the genesis and preparation of the original edition: Helen Field; Ernst Hug; Nigel Jackson; K. Frank Jensen; Prudence Jones; Barbara Meyer; the late Colin Murray; Rosemarie Kirschmann; Sean Pennick; Cambridge University Library; St. Fagans National Museum of History, Wales; National Museum of Ireland, Dublin; British Museum, London; Pitt Rivers Museum, Oxford; Württembergisches Landesmuseum, Stuttgart; and the Fastnachtsmuseum Narrenschopf, Bad Dürrheim. A particular thanks to Michael Moynihan for his meticulous editing of this revised edition.

The Celtic spiritual landscape is present at all levels of being.

Celtic Tree Alphabets, Ancient and Modern

This is a substantially revised edition of my book *Ogham and Coelbren*, written 1998–99 and published in 2000. It was originally intended as an expansion of earlier works that I had published on Bardo-Druidic alphabets in the 1970s and 1980s. From my teens I had seen ancient stones bearing Ogham inscriptions in museums and standing in their original locations in the west of England, Wales, and Ireland. In the 1960s, when I first became interested in esoteric matters, it was not like the present where vast numbers of rare books are digitized and available online. I had to go to libraries in person and rummage through shelves containing books that had often been unperused for decades. Access to old books in libraries revealed to me works on Druidic occultism, including texts by nineteenth-century Scottish and Irish writers. From a bookseller in Aberystwyth, Wales, I obtained a rare first volume of *Barddas* (1862), which purported to be an encyclopedic treatise on ancient Welsh lore. The later authors Dudley Wright (1924) and Lewis Spence (1945) revealed Bardic alphabets whose provenance they did not explain.

In the 1970s, various esoteric groups in Britain investigated the Ogham tree sequence, and at the alternative fairs held at Rougham in Suffolk (in which I participated), a tree alphabet circle composed of the corresponding woods was erected as a sacred enclosure. The Golden Section Order, whose driving force was Colin Murray (1942–1986), published between the mid-1970s and 1980s numerous booklets and papers that explored the relationship between the Ogham tree characters and the cycles of the seasons, though in certain pentagrams he used to explain solar and lunar mysteries, "bird Ogham" correspondences also appeared.

The term *alphabet* is used in this book for convenience even though the letters of the scripts do not follow the order from which that word is derived. Technically, an alphabet is a character row beginning with the letters A (*alpha*), B (*beta*), and so forth, as in Greek, Roman, or Hebrew, for example. Conventionally, however, it has become a generic word for letter rows in general, whatever order they may have, and that is how it should be understood. It should also be acknowledged that the "tree alphabets" dealt with here are contentious in several ways, though Ogham as understood today in esoteric circles especially is a standardized form with tree ascriptions, which has spread since the 1970s through Druidic communities worldwide.

The Ogham lore described in this book is based upon authentic Irish texts of various dates, including the medieval *Auraicept na n-Éces* (Scholars' Primer) from *The Book of Ballymote* and the much later seventeeth-century work of O'Flaherty, *Ogygia*. Although contemporary Ogham writings generally use standard tree names, and this book is about that system, anciently it was more than that. The most ancient Irish texts about Ogham are variable and contradictory in their ascriptions, as indeed the many versions of Ogham in *The Book of Ballymote* (which also includes runes) show, and there are completely different ones for many characters that have nothing to do with trees. Not until the medieval period were the Oghams associated more systematically with trees (and some non-woody plants).

Modern scholarship would level severe criticism at any claim of a primordial tree-only Ogham system. Already in the late nineteenth century, Charles Graves asserted that it was wrong to regard all Irish letter names as trees (1876, 459): "It can be shown with almost certainty of proof that *nin, huat, tinne, muin, gort, straif, ur, oir, uillenn,* and *emancoll,* are not the Irish names of trees and plants." Much more recently, Damian McManus asserted that many of the Ogham ascriptions were a "figment of the medieval Irish glossators' imagination" (1988, 128).

Also, various ancient texts called *Bríatharogaim* (Speech Oghams), which appear to have been a teaching aid, preserve kennings for each Ogham. While a few of these kennings are arboreal, they speak only in vague terms of a "most exalted tree," "fairest tree," "discerning tree," and so forth. By contrast, the majority of the kennings have no arboreal sense at all. For example, the Ogham *Huath,* which is now ascribed to the Thorn tree, possesses with respect to its variant form *Úath* (the Irish word for "fear") three kennings of frightening and dangerous things: an "assembly of packs of hounds," a "blanching of faces," and something "most difficult at night." *Ur,* which is—depending on the source—ascribed to Ling (Heather), Blackthorn, or Honeysuckle, has three kennings that refer instead to earth or soil: "in cold dwellings" and the "shroud of a lifeless one," both of which refer to the buried dead, and a "propagation of plants" (McManus 1988, 137). Each Ogham character has its own kennings, none of which name specific trees.

The tree-alphabet ascriptions that are well evident in the Ogham tract of the *Auraicept na n-Éces* received additional modern impetus from the presentation of Ogham in Roderic O'Flaherty's *Ogygia* (1793), which was originally published in Latin in 1685. The arboreal correspondences were then popularized and expanded upon by the poet Robert Graves in his book *The White Goddess* (1949), and further refined by writers who followed Graves. And it was Graves who was a seminal influence of what became the pagan movement, especially its Celtic tendency. It should also be noted that the characters of the Gaelic alphabet, used in both the Irish and Scots versions of the language, are ascribed tree names that correspond to the names used in standard Ogham, and this usage goes back at least to the eighteenth century.

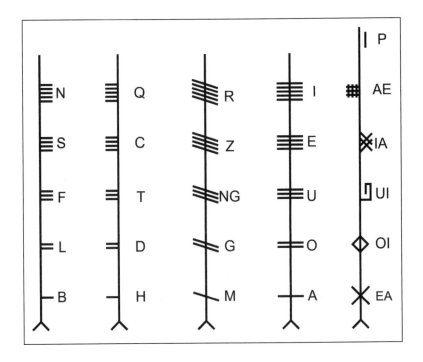

COELBREN Y BEIRDD, HERWYDD DOSPARTH LLAWDDEN.

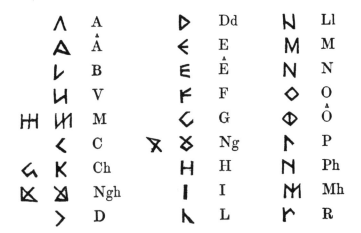

Above: The ancient Ogham alphabet (Wikimedia Commons).
Below: Iolo Morganwg's Coelbren alphabet as presented in
John Williams Ab Ithel's *Barddas* (1862).

Unlike Ogham, whose ancient inscriptions on stones in Ireland and western Britain attest to its antiquity, the origin of the Welsh "Bardic alphabet" called Coelbren is much more contentious. Dating to the early nineteenth century, but claimed to predate that, there are no examples of it prior to supposed transcriptions produced by the Bard Iolo Morganwg (Edward Williams, 1747–1826). A grammatical text called *Dosparth Edeyrn Davod Aur*, translated by the Reverend John Williams Ab Ithel and published in 1856, is supposed to have been authored by a thirteenth-century Welsh Bard, but identified by the National Library of Wales to be spurious, having been written by Lewis Richards in 1821 and derived from one of Iolo's manuscripts. In addition to the Coelbren Bardic letters, *Dosparth Edeyrn Davod Aur* contains several other allegedly ancient scripts: the Alphabet of Nemnivus; the *Coelbren y meneich* ("Monkish Alphabet"); and the "Winged Alphabet" that has two rows of twig-runes of the Younger Futhark, which the author clearly knew nothing about. To these, Lewis Spence added the supposed Druidic alphabets of Beth–Luis–Nion and Bobileth, possibly arcane magical alphabets arranged more or less in the Ogham sequence.*

Iolo appears to have been somewhat of a rascal. Nevertheless, his influence over later developments of the Celtic mysteries is significant. Reformers of old religions and philosophies, as well as inspired prophets and inventers of new ones—some of them frauds—have existed for thousands of years. It is difficult to distinguish between these categories, as many true-believer devotees claim that their founder spoke the "one-and-only truth," and that all else is error. Some are historic and some are legendary or even fictional. They include Zoroaster, Orpheus, Moses, the Buddha, Odin, the Emperor Augustus, Togo Dubellinus, Saint Paul, Guru Nanak, John Wesley, Emanuel Swedenborg, Henry Hurle, Joseph Smith, Mary Baker Eddy, Madame Blavatsky, Gerald Gardner, and L. Ron Hubbard, to name but a few. Foundation myths,

---

*Only Ogham and Coelbren are discussed in the present book.

however fanciful, appear in numerous initiation rituals of religions and mystic orders. The work of Iolo Morganwg is the foundation of a current of Druidry that stems from the orders of the nineteenth century. William Blake, whom later Druids claimed without evidence as chief of one of the many Druidic orders, claimed that anything that it is possible to believe is an image of the truth, and Iolo proved that.

The illustrations in this book are part of my Celtic Art corpus,* and many were specially drawn for the first edition. The infinitely variable threads of Celtic Art coalesce in flowing patterns that interlace and spiral, echoing the entangled thickets of the wildwood; the weavings of fate; and the fluid flow of wind, water, and spirit. It is an art that embodies the metaphorical and analogical view of the world that emerges from the spiritual landscapes of the Celtic lands.

The symbolic green man of the wildwood may wrestle with mythic beasts; he may be a sylvan, shamanic figure like Merlin or the Green Man, who is half man, half tree. New identities appear in the wildwood. The roebuck may hide in the thicket, but equally, the tangled wood can conceal fatal danger. We must enter the vague terrain if we wish to find certain spiritual truths "vivid as the forms of nature . . . a fountain of interior light" as Æ (George Russell) wrote of in *A Mythic Vision* (A. E. 1918, 28). Bardic creativity has made new visions such as the Awen of Menw and the wooden rack of letters, but even these fanciful images are significant in modern Druidry and have their place in the ever-evolving story of Celtic spirituality. For it is through the interlaced knotwork that we may find a path, if we are brave enough.

---

*My work has been featured in the book *New Visions in Celtic Art*, edited by David James and Stuart Booth (1999), and exhibited at the Birmingham (England) City Library in 2002 and in the *Celtic Art Worldwide* show at the Walkers' Gallery, San Marcos, Texas in 2017.

1

The Irish Tree Alphabet

THE ORIGIN AND A BRIEF OVERVIEW OF OGHAM

The form of writing known as Ogham or Ogam [pronounced *OH-um*] was used in historic times in Ireland and the western parts of ancient Britain. Its precise age is uncertain, though some have claimed that it was in existence as early as 2200 BCE. Historically, however, according to Professor Brendan O'Hehir of the University of California at Berkeley, the earliest dateable Ogham is from around the second century CE. Also, it is certain that the majority of definite Ogham inscriptions are located in Ireland, with smaller numbers found in Wales, the Isle of Man, and England (Cornwall and Devon).

Early modern researchers into Ogham at first claimed that it was derived from Greek sources, even Hellenic semaphore that used blazing torches, but, more recently, the Latin (Roman) alphabet has been favored as its base. Several hundred ancient Ogham inscriptions are known to exist. They have been found on rockfaces, standing stones, Celtic crosses, portable artifacts, and in manuscripts. In 1945 R. A. S. Macalister published the *Corpus Inscriptionum Insularum Celticarum*, a collection of every known Ogham inscription on stone from the British Isles. There were 385 in all. Most of them (320) are in Ireland, of which 130 are in County Kerry (60 are from the

1

Dingle Peninsula alone), 84 in Cork, 48 in Waterford, and the rest scattered through Leinster and the eastern seaboard.* The Barony of Corca Dhuibhne (which corresponds to the Dingle Peninsula), where Ogham stones are most numerous, is a kind of archaic origin place where, according to legendary history, all manner of significant changes were first introduced to Ireland.

Most of the other ancient Ogham stones are in places where Irish invasions and colonization took place: the Isle of Man, Scotland, Wales, and the former Dumnonia (Cornwall and Devon). Between the third and sixth centuries CE, there were continued invasions of Great Britain from Ireland. Irish invasions of western Britain were extensive. They involved relatively short occupations of parts of what is now Wales and Cornwall, and a permanent conquest of Caledonia (north Britain) by the Scots who originated in the north of Ireland.

The medieval Irish narrative known as "The Expulsion of the Déisi" tells how, around the year 265 CE, accompanied by his family and followers, Eochaid, son of Artchorp, invaded the territory of Demed (Dyfed, Wales). There, "his sons and grandsons died"; from them came the "Race of Crimthann" (Meyer 1901, 113). Cormac's ninth-century-CE *Glossary* also mentions Irish incursions into Great Britain:

> For when great was the power of the Gael [Irish] on Britain, they divided Alba between them into districts, and each knew the residence of his friend, and not less did the Gael dwell on the east side of the sea quam in Scotia [Ireland], and their habitations and royal forts were built there. . . . Thus every tribe divided on that side, for its property to the east [Great Britain] was equal [to that on the west (i.e., Ireland)] and they continue in this power till long after the coming of Patrick. (O'Donovan 1868, 111)

---

*Since the publication of Macalister's *Corpus*, the total number has risen slightly, to around 400.

Ogham standing stone from County Kerry, Ireland,
with Pagan and Christian symbols.

In the sixth century, the dynasty of the ethnic British (Welsh), Brythonic-speaking Cunedda ruled north Wales, while the south was ruled by Goidelic-speaking ethnic Irish. The boundary lay roughly along a line between the Dee and the Teifi rivers. The Ogham stones in Wales are certainly the product of these Irish colonies. Around fifty have been noted. Most are inscribed with Christian texts in Latin as well as Irish Ogham. By the style of the accompanying Roman letters, most date from the fifth and sixth centuries CE, generally before the year 550.

The Ogham stones are Irish memorials, inscribed with a formula: the name of the dead person is always given in its genitive form, inferring "the grave of" or "the stone of." Some stones give a single name, while others record the deceased's patrilinearity. A stone from Nevern in Pembrokeshire is typical, reading: MAGLICUNAS MAQI CLUTARI, the "stone (or grave) of Maglicu Mac [son of] Clutarius." Another, at Brynkir in Caernarvonshire, carries only a single name, Icorigas, meaning the "stone (or grave) of Icorix." Instead of MAQI, "son of," some Ogham inscriptions have AVI, "grandson" or "descendent of," or INGENIA, "daughter of."

Because Ogham was an Irish form of writing, it died out in Wales when most ethnic Irish were exterminated, and the survivors expelled, during the Welsh resurgence of the seventh century. For many years, one of the landmarks for sailors on the Irish Sea was a vast cairn of Irish skulls heaped up on a headland at Holyhead in Anglesey. In Caledonia, the Irish conquest was permanent. The indigenous Picts were largely exterminated, and the survivors absorbed, while the British (Welsh) were expelled from Strathclyde, and Scotland came into being.

Although the majority of the ancient surviving inscriptions are memorials, various medieval and later texts indicate that the Ogham alphabet also had a symbolic aspect. When Christian missionaries introduced the Roman alphabet to Ireland, and, later, Scandinavian settlers brought the runes, these scripts—and not Ogham—were preferred for memorials. In Ireland and western Britain, there are monuments upon which both Ogham and Roman letters coexist. By the end of the sixth century, Ogham had gone out of use on public monuments. However, by the ninth century, craftsmen had begun to use Ogham *feadha* ("characters" or "letters" [but literally "trees"] also spelled *feda*; sg. *fidh* or *fid*).

Some of the Ogham stones on the Isle of Man, Scotland, and Shetland are later than those in the rest of Britain, dating from the tenth to the twelfth centuries. Their inscriptions are known among Oghamists as "scholastic Oghams," which are also found on metal artifacts from monasteries and the courts of kings and lords. This type of Ogham differs from the earlier form because the feadha are cut across an engraved line, not the *arris* (edge) of the stone (see chap. 2).

Scholastic Oghams are in the style of manuscript Ogham texts. The only inscriptions from mainland Europe that have any reason to be called Ogham date from this time, when Irish monks traveled Central Europe and founded monasteries following the Celtic Christian rule. Scholastic Oghams are defined as dating between the ninth and seventeenth century. Contemporary Oghams are a continuation of the "scholastic" tradition by way of manuscripts and the researches of antiquaries of the eighteenth and nineteenth centuries.

In addition to their use by "scholars," Oghams were part of the vernacular learning of the "Plain People of Ireland," too.* History provides sporadic instances: for example, in the nineteenth century, a man surnamed Collins was brought before a magistrate in County Cork because he had not painted his name on his cart, as required by law. He was able to explain that his name *was* on the cart—written in Ogham—and was acquitted. The nineteenth-century antiquary John Windle carried a stick inscribed with Ogham. He and the parish priest of Blarney, the Reverend Matthew Horgan, were avid preservers of Ogham learning.

An Irish vernacular rhyme mentioned by O'Begly and MacCurtin in 1732 and recorded (in English) by collectors in the nineteenth century began:

---

*I am using the phrase the "Plain People of Ireland" popularized by the satirical-comic Irish writer Brian O'Nolan (1911–1966) whose nom de plume was Flann O' Brien.

For B one stroke at your right hand,
And L doth always two demand.
For F draw three; for S make four;
When you want N, you add one more . . .

(FERGUSON 1887, 12)

This country rhyme contains the description of all of the Ogham feadha and how they are written. It was the key by which the antiquaries, first of all the Right Reverend Bishop Graves, were able to decipher ancient Ogham inscriptions.

In the middle of the nineteenth century, "Celtic Revival" artifacts became popular among the ruling class in Ireland and Britain.* They included the Clarendon Shawl Brooch otherwise called the "Ogham Pin." Made by the jewelers Waterhouse and Company from 1849 onward, this was a replica of the Ballyspellan Brooch, a medieval Celtic artifact with scholastic Ogham inscriptions on the reverse side. Waterhouse offered these brooches either in gold with Irish pearls, silver, or silver gilt inlaid with Bog Oak. These copies of the Ballyspellan Brooch brought Ogham to public attention for the first time since the early medieval period.

During the twentieth century, the poet Robert Graves further popularized Ogham through his book *The White Goddess* (1947), where he interpreted ancient Celtic poetry in the light of the "Tree Alphabet." This gave an impetus to the esoteric study of Ogham, which was further refined in the 1970s in England by Colin Murray in his Druidic organization called the Golden Section Order. Murray was the first person to put Ogham into the form of divination cards. Since then, Ogham has become an integral part of the teachings of Celtic spirituality.

---

*In common with several other national bodies that were subsumed into larger states (such as Finland, Norway, Brittany, Catalonia, Frisia, and Hungary), which sought to assert their separate identities through ancient art and literature, from the late eighteenth century, Ireland and Celtic parts of Britain began to assert their cultural identity separate from the ruling mainstream. They restored local traditional forms of art, music, and language, and created a characteristic cultural system, which in Ireland and Britain was called the Celtic Revival (or Celtic Twilight).

This brief history of Ogham demonstrates that it has developed over time from carvings on the edges of standing stones to bookish and metal forms and finally divination cards. The interpretation of the meanings of the individual feadha have also varied and developed through their history. Apart from their phonetic meanings, we do not know what esoteric significance the earliest Ogham had. Later manuscripts, especially the fourteenth-century *Book of Ballymote*, give us full descriptions of numerous esoteric correspondences, which may or may not have existed earlier. Other commentaries exist in the Old Irish text called *Auraicept na n-Éces* (modern Irish *Uraiceacht na nÉigeas*, variously translated as "The Scholars' Primer" or "The Precepts of the Poets"). This tells how the autonomous colleges of Druidry and Bardism, and also independent Bards, developed individual and variant systems of correspondences for the Ogham feadha. These correspondences are in turn developed, reinterpreted, and sometimes contradicted by later texts.

More recently, the twentieth-century commentators added their own interpretations in line with modern scholarship, in some cases modifying and changing earlier ascriptions. All of these forms attest to the dynamic continuous development of Ogham for the best part of two millennia. As with all dynamic systems, there has never been a fixed point in history that states: "This is definitive." However, Ogham does have a recognizable "spirit," which, although it is not a simple thing to define it precisely, has determined the past history and the present uses of the "Celtic Tree Alphabet."

LEGENDARY ORIGINS: OGMA GRIANAINECH

The legendary Irish orator-warrior figure named Ogma is referred to in the ancient narrative *Cath Maige Tuired* (The Second Battle of Mag Tuired) as one of the supernatural Tuatha Dé Danann, along with Dagda and Lugh. In the *Táin Bó Cúailnge* (Cattle Raid of Cooley) a hero named Ogma Grianainech ("Ogma the Sun-faced") is described as one of the warriors of Ulster. According to the *Book of Ballymote*, Ogma was the son of Elathan, and brother of Breass MacElathan, the *ardrí* (high king) of all Ireland.

The Ballyspellan Brooch, front and back,
with scholastic Ogham inscriptions.

Ogma Grianainech MacElathan bears a forename similar to that of a Gaulish god. In his dialogue on Heracles (Hercules), the Greek author Lucian mentions Ogmios as the Celtic equivalent to the Greco-Roman demigod. He describes an image he saw in Gaul that showed Ogmios as a dark-skinned old man, clad in a lion's skin and carrying a club and a bow. Chains of amber and gold emanated from the tip of his tongue to bind the ears of captives, who followed him willingly.

Lucian was told that Ogmios personified the power of eloquence and wisdom, which only develops fully in old age. A god called Ogmios is also known from two Latin-inscribed tablets found in Bregenz (Brigantium), an old Celtic center in the Austrian state of Vorarlberg. There, he appears with the underworldly deities Dis Pater and Aeracura, and is assumed to be a psychopomp or guide of the dead in the underworld like they are. The golden chains described by Lucian appear as golden rays in a Romano-British image of Ogmios, echoing the Irish epithet of Ogma as "Sun-faced." Also, a fragment of pottery found at Richborough (Rutupiae) depicts a god with rays coming from the head and a whip in his hand, with the inscription *Ogmia*.

According to the tract on Ogham in the *Book of Ballymote* (fol. 308–314), Ogma, the epitome of eloquence and wisdom, was the legendary inventor of the Ogham alphabet. Irish texts depict Ogma as a champion warrior who is skilled in languages to the point of originating a dialect and a script.

The *Auraicept na n-Éces* recounts how Ogma employed a twig of Birch to carve the first Oghams. It carried a message to Lug mac Etlenn ("Lug, son of Ethliu"), telling him that his wife would be abducted seven times into the Otherworld "unless birch guard her" (Calder 1917, 273–75). The Ogham carving consisted of seven single strokes to the left of the *druim,** seven Bs. This story appears to be an origin myth

---

*The *druim* is the center line or "ridge" of an Ogham inscription (see chap. 2, "Ogham Terminology"). It is a topographical term, present in Irish place names such as Drumcree and Drumcondra.

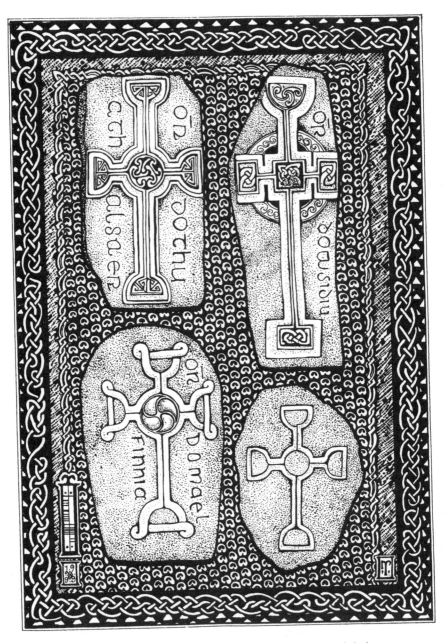

Early medieval Irish mentorial slabs with Gaeilge alphabet
inscriptions. Clockwise from top left: stone of the smith Tuathall Saer at
Clonmacnoise, County Offaly; stone of Algidu, Durrow, County Offaly;
uninscribed cross-slab, Clonmacnoise; slab dedicated to
Máel Finnia, Clonmacnoise.

to explain the primacy of the Birch in the Oghams. According to the *Book of Ballymote*, Ogma's intention in inventing Ogham was as a secret cipher, "for signs of secret speech only known to the learned, and designed to be kept from the vulgar and poor of the nation" (Atkinson 1874, 207). Corroborating this use are the 150 different varieties of Ogham recorded in the *Book of Ballymote*.

The Irish bishop and king, Cormac, in his tenth-century CE *Glossary*, recounts how the Oghams were used by the early Pagan Irish before the time of Saint Patrick and his followers. He tells of the "mete-wand" or measuring rod used to measure bodies for burials, on which "the people wrote in *Oghuim* [Ogham] whatever was hateful or detestable relating to them, and left it in the cemetery" (Atkinson 1874, 205). In Chapter xiv of *The English Irish Dictionary*, titled "Of the Ancient Characters called *ogham*, and of the Abbreviations call'd *nodaighe*," O'Begly and MacCurtin write (1732, 714):

> The Irish Antiquaries preserv'd this *Ogam* in particular, as a piece of the greatest value in all their Antiquity. And it was penal for any but those that were sworn Antiquaries either to study or use that same. For in these Characters those sworn Antiquaries wrote all the evil actions and other vicious practices of their Monarchs and great personages both male and female; that it should not be known to any but to themselves and their successours being sworn Antiquaries . . .

A parallel to this keeping of secret records of "evil acts" is practiced in south Germany to this day by certain masked participants in the Swabian-Alemannic *Fastnacht* (with dialectal variants such as *Fasnacht*, *Fasnet*, etc.) ceremonies around Shrovetide. Called *Schandtle*, they carry small books recording such deeds, and whisper them in disguised voices to the individuals concerned. The historic connection with earlier times is uncertain, but the function of Bards, Jesters, and Fools often overlaps in traditional society.

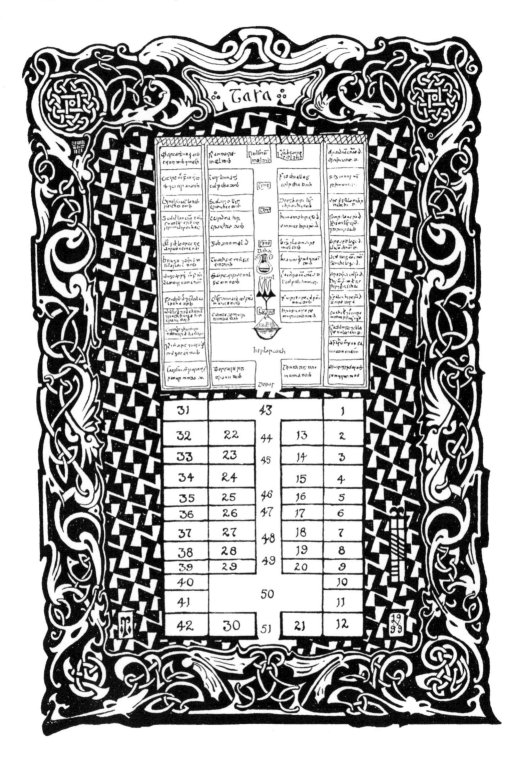

Historical Records of Ogham

The oldest Irish historical stories contain many references to the Ogham alphabet, often as sepulchral memorials. In the *Lebor na hUidre* (Book of the Dun Cow), for example, the grave of the third-century CE king Fothad Airgthech is said to have had *Fothad Airgthech ind so*, "FOTHAD AIRGTHECH HERE" inscribed in Oghams (O'Donovan 1845, xlv). The story of Deirdre tells of her joint tomb with Naisi: "Their stone was raised over their monument, their Ogham names were written, and their ceremony of lamentation was performed." In a poem recorded in the *Book of Leinster*, we are told of "Ogham on the stone, the stone over the monument" at the site of a battle fought in the third century CE:

Opposite: Layout of the great hall of the high kings of Ireland at Tara according to the *Yellow Book of Lecan*, showing ritual seating positions of the classes of ancient Irish society (south at the top): 1. Charioteers and Stewards; 2. Deerstalkers; 3. Airs Foraill (first-grade nobility); 4. High King and Queen; 5. Aire Ard (third-grade nobility) and Cli (third-grade poets); 6. Aire Tusi (second-grade nobility) and Historians; 7. Aire Desa (fourteenth-grade nobility) and Dos (fifth-grade poets); 8. Fochloc (sixth-grade poets); 9. Cooks; 10. Fortress engineers; 11. Champions and Cane (fourth-grade poets); 12. Sappers; 13. Board-game players; 14. Spencers; 15. Braziers; 16. Physicians; 17. Pilots; 18. Merchants; 19. Jesters; 20. Buffoons; 21. King's Fools; 22. Flute players; 23. Schoolteachers; 24. Goldsmiths; 25. Smiths; 26. Shield-makers; 27. Chariot-wrights; 28. Conjurors; 29. Satirists; 30. Doorkeepers; 31. Horsemen; 32. Harpers and Drummers; 33. Judges; 34. Doctors of Letters and their nominated successors; 35. Chief Poets and Anrwith (second-grade poets); 36. Hospitalers; 37. Master Wrights and their successors; 38. Soothsayers and Druids; 39. Builders and Wrights; 40. Pipers and Trumpeters; 41. Engravers; 42. Cordwainers; 43. Servants; 44, 45, 46. Hearths; 47. Cauldron; 48. Candlestick; 49. Lantern; 50. Common Hall; 51. Door.

That Ogham which is on the stone,
Around which many were slain;
If Finn of the many battles lived,
Long would the Ogham be remembered.

(O'DONOVAN 1845, XLV)

From texts and from extant memorials in Ireland and Wales, it appears that the Oghams carved on stone monuments usually contained only the names of those commemorated. But as the *Auraicept na n-Éces* records, Oghams carved on wood could have a magical or secret function. The *Lebor na hUidre*, a manuscript dating from the early twelfth century, contains the story of the *Táin Bó Cúailnge* (Cattle Raid of Cooley). In it, the hero Cú Chulainn cuts an Ogham on willow withies that he bends into a hoop. These are interpreted by Fergus in the army of Queen Medb (Atkinson 1874, 204). The story of the exile of the sons of Duil Dermait tells how Cú Chulainn inscribes Oghams on a spear, giving it talismanic powers. The *Book of Leinster* also tells of the exile of Corc, who was driven out by his father, Lughaidh, king of Munster. Arriving in Caledonia, Corc was recognized by Gruibné, bard of King Feradach. Examining Corc's shield, the bard discovered an Ogham inscription on it, the ominous meaning of which Corc was ignorant (Atkinson 1874, 205).

In addition to inscriptions upon stone, the ancient Irish reckoned four other ways of writing the Oghams. They are: *Tamlorga filidh*, "Staves of the Poets"; *Tabhall lorga*, "Tablet Staves"; *Fleasc fili*, the "Wand of the Poet"; and *Taibhli filidh*, "Tablets of the Poets" (Atkinson 1874, 204). The exact form of the *Taibhli filidh* is unknown. However, descriptions of them suggest they may have been similar to certain ancient runic calendars known from Scandinavia. These are in the form of a wooden fan, which, when closed, looked something like a baton or staff. The traditional Irish law code known as the Brehon Laws gives the privilege or "badge of office" of a poet as a *Tabhall lorg* ("Tablet staff").

The story of Bailé Mac Buain, "the Sweet Spoken," the favorite lover of Aillinn, tells how some of them came into being. At the place where they were buried, an Apple and a Yew tree grew on their graves (Q and I in Ogham). After seven years, the seers of Ulster cut down the Yew that grew over Bailé and made a *Tabhall fileadh* ("Poets' Tablet") from it. On the tablet, they wrote "the visions, and espousals, and loves, and the courtships of Ulster" (Atkinson 1874, 204).

They also cut down the Apple of Aillinn, and on the tablet made from its wood, they inscribed the visions, marriages, loves, and courtships of Leinster. These tablets finally ceased to be usable in the time of King Art, son of Conn of the Hundred Battles (166 CE). At the feast of Samhain, as was customary, the bards and professors of all the arts gathered together at the king's court to read from their tablets. The tablets of Baile and Aillinn were given to Art, but, as he was reading them, suddenly they closed together, and could never again be separated (Atkinson 1874, 204–5).

Ogham in the Book of Ballymote

The most important source of Ogham is the *Book of Ballymote*, a major text written at Ballymote in the county of Sligo in the house of Tomaltach Og Mac Donough, Lord of Corann. It dates from the time that Torlough Og, the son of Hugh O'Conor, was king of Connacht. Charles O'Conor of Belanagar later inserted the date 1391 (on fol. 62b). The *Book of Ballymote* is composed of 252 leaves of vellum in the large folio format (10 x 13.5 inches or 26.67 x 34.29 cm). Its pages were transcribed by several hands, mainly by Solomon O'Droma and Manus O'Duigenann. The text is a compilation of various material from older manuscripts. It commences with a version of the *Lebor Gabála Érenn* (Book of Invasions of Ireland).

Following this are several chronologies and historical episodes in poetry and prose. After them come the genealogies of Irish saints and the notable tribes and families of the Milesian race, the acts of various kings, and other episodes from Irish mythological history. The aforementioned treatise on ancient Irish grammar and prosody, *Auraicept na n-Éces*, is ascribed to Fercertne, the chief *fili* (Bard) of the king of Ulster, Conor Mac Nessa, and enlarged around 628 CE by Cennfaeladh, son of Ailill. Next, and most importantly for our purposes, there is an illustrated treatise on the Ogham alphabets of the ancient Irish. The book ends with a text on the adventures of Aeneas after the fall of Troy.

In the section headed "Oghaim na nGadhel" (The Irish Oghaims [Oghams]), the *Book of Ballymote* gives the following explanation in the traditional catechismal question-and-answer form:

From whence, what time, and what person, and from what cause, did the Oghaim [Ogham] spring? Answer: The place is Hybernia's Ile, which we Scots inhabit; in the time of Breas, the son of Elathan, then king of all Ireland. The person was Ogma, the son of Elathan, the son of Dealbadh, brother to Breas, for Breas, Ogma, and Dealbadh were three sons of Elathan, who was the son of Dealbath.

Ogma, being a man much skilled in dialects and in poetry, it was he who invented the Ogham, its object being for signs of secret speech only known to the learned, and designed to be kept from the vulgar and poor of the nation.

Where were the names and figures of the Oghaim found? Who were the mother and the father of the Oghaim? What was the first name written in Oghaim characters? What tree was it written in? Why was it written? What was written? And from whom came the art of numbering and forming books regularly in Oghaim? It is called Ogham from Ogma, the inventor. The derivation is Oghaim, from Ghuaim, i.e., the *guaim*, or wisdom through which the bards were enabled to compose;* for by its branches the Irish bards sounded their verses. The father of Ogham was Ogma, and the mother of Ogham was the hand or knife of Ogma. *Soim* was the first thing written in Ogham. . . . In a birch was it written, and given to Lug, the son of Etlem, with an explanation multiply-

---

*This can be seen as equivalent to the Welsh *awen*, a term for poetic or bardic inspiration.

ing branches, which ran as from the roots, namely: seven slips in one sheaf slip . . . and gave them folded, entitled male and female, another name, man or woman, of the birch; for of the birch they first wrote Oghaims.

How many and what are the divisions of Ogham? Four; B, her five; H, her five; M, her five; and A, her five.

How many sciences in the Ogham are taught, and what are they? Answer:

Three: VIII royal or gentle trees; VIII kiln trees; and VIII spiral trees. The VIII royal trees are the elm, oak, hazel, vine, ivy, blackthorn, broom, spine; and the VIII kiln are the birch, the quicken, willow, ash, whitethorn, fig, apple, and cork; and the spiral are all from green trees.*

How many kinds of Ogham are there? Answer: 150, *Figuras eorum et potestates per ordinem nunciabimus* [We will announce their shapes and powers in order]. First, the branches of the trees are they from whence come the names of the branches in Ogham, *per alios & alios nominator* [by others and others it is named].

Question: By whom and from whence are the veins and beams in the Ogham tree named?

Answer. . . . It came from the school of Phenius . . . through the world, teaching the tongues (he thus employed), in number 25. Noble youths (or 25 noble schools through the world).

From whence come the figures and names in the explanation of B, L, and N in Ogham?

Answer: From the branches and limbs of the oak tree: they formed ideas which they expressed in sounds, i.e., as the stalk of the bush is the noblest part; from them they formed the seven chief figures as vowels . . . and they formed three others, which they added to these as helpers, formed on different sides

---

*Other lists, from the *Auraicept na n-Éces* and Brehon Law, give different ascriptions; see Appendices 1 and 2.

of the line *per alios*, the branches of the wood give figures for the branches and veins in Ogham, chief of all. The tribe of B, from birch, and the daughter, i.e., the ash of the wood, is chief; and of them the first alphabet was formed; of L, namely L, from *luis*, the quicken tree of the wood; F, from *fearn*, alder, good for shields; S from *sail*, a willow from the wood; N, in Ogham, from *nin*, the ash, for spears; H, in Ogham from *uath*, whitethorn, a crooked tree, or a bush, because of her thorns; D, from *dur*, the Oak of fate from the wood; T, from *tine*, Cypress, or from the Elder Tree; C, in Ogham from *coll*, the hazel of the wood; Q, in Ogham of *quert*, apple, aspen or mountain ash; M, from *mediu* (muin), the vine branching finely; G, from *gort*, namely ivy tower-ing; NG, from *getal*, or *gilcach*, a reed; ST or Z, from *draighean*, blackthorn; R, Graif [not explained]; A, from *ailm*, fir; O, from *on*, the broom, furze; U, from *ur*, Heath; E, from *edadh*, aspen trem-bling; I from *ida*, or *ioda*, or *ioga*, the yew tree; EA, *eabhadh*, the aspen; OI, *oir*, the spine; UI, *inlleann*, honeysuckle; IO, the Goose-berry (*ifin*; Æ, the witch hazel (*amhancholl*); Pine, Ogham, that is the divine pine from the wood, from whence are drawn the four *ifins*, or vineyards, *per alios*, the name of that branch. The figure resembles the hurdle of wrought twigs, or like a bier. (Atkinson 1874, 207–9; translation slightly edited)

Clearly, a major intention of Ogham's creator was to make a code that could be used to conceal information from those who were not supposed to have it. However, unlike the modern era, when codes exist solely as utilitarian means of keeping information secret, the ancient Celts had no concept of plain utilitarianism. Because they had an ensouled worldview, nothing that they produced was seen as separate, reflecting the complex interactions of things in the world. Thus, with Ogham, while remaining very serviceable as a code, it is also a philosophical system in its own right. Although they were chosen arbitrarily—that is, any number or disposition of strokes could have denoted any letter—the originator chose to base the individual characters on trees. The names of the trees already existed, and their initial letters were thus fixed. The qualities and uses of the trees were also fixed. But the order in which the characters were arranged, and their interactive meaning with one another, were created anew when Ogham came into being. With such a code, it is possible to convey vast arrays of meaning through very simple symbols.

Later Developments and Modern Systems

Most contemporary interpretations of Ogham are derived from the seventeenth-century Irish Bard and historian Ruaidhri Ó Flaithbheartaigh (Roderic O'Flaherty, 1629–1718). In his book *Ogygia, or a Chronological Account of Irish Events*, which was written in Latin and only published in an English translation by the Rev. James Hely in 1793, he ascribes the invention of alphabets to "The person Forchern, the philosopher Fenius Farfaidh [who] composed the first alphabets of the Hebrews, the Greeks, the Latins, and Bethluisnin an Oghuim" (O'Flaherty 1793, 2:III, 83). Also, he wrote:

> Mr. Ware says as follows in his *Irish Antiquities*, chap. 2: "Besides the common characters, the ancient Irish used various occult or artificial methods of writing, called *Ogum*, in which they wrote their secret and mysterious affairs. I have a book filled with them. The letters themselves were anciently called *Feadha*, i.e., woods." (O'Flaherty 1793, 2:III, 99, punctuation modified)

O'Flaherty's interpretations have been criticized by several prominent Oghamists, especially R. A. S. Macalister. They note that the ascriptions given by O'Flaherty and his followers differed significantly from those in the *Book of Ballymote*, calling them late inventions that have little relationship to the "original" meanings.

In his *Ogygia*, O'Flaherty listed the Ogham ("Virgean") characters as: B *Beithe*, the Birch tree; L *Luis*, commonly *Caertheann*, the wild Ash; F *Fearn*, the Alder; S *Sail*, the Willow; N *Nion*, vulgarly *Unfionn*, the Ash tree; H *Huath* (*Sce*), White-thorn or thorny bushes that grow on hedges; D *Duir*, vulgarly *Cuileann*, the Scarlet Oak, Broom, Holm, Holly; T *Tinne*, "the explanation of this letter is not given"; C *Coll*, the "Hazle"; Q *Queirt*, vulgarly *Abholl*, the Apple tree; M *Muin*, vulgarly *Fineamhuin*, the Vine tree; G *Gort*, vulgarly *Fidheann*, the Ivy; Ng *Ngedal*, vulgarly *Gilcach* or *Raid*, the Reed; P *Pethpoc*, "no explanation"; Z *Ztraif,* vulgarly *Draighean*, the Sloe tree; R *Ruis*, vulgarly *Trom*, the Alder tree; A *Ailm*, vulgarly *Gius*, the Fir tree; O *Onn*, vulgarly *Aiteann*, Furze; U *Ur*, vulgarly *Fræch*, Heath or Ling; E *Eadhadh*, vulgarly Cranncriothach, the Aspen tree; I *Idho* or *Idhad*, vulgarly *Ibhar*, the Yew tree; Ra *Ehhadh*, vulgarly *Criothach*, the Aspen tree; O *Oir*, vulgarly *Feoras*; the Spindle tree or Prickwood; Y *Uilleann*, vulgarly *Eadhleann*, Woodbine, Honeysuckle; Io *Iphin*, vulgarly *Spinan* or *Ispin*, the Gooseberry tree; X *Amhancholl*, "I do not know the meaning of it." (O'Flaherty 1793, 2: III, 102–3)

O'Flaherty's system was very influential among esoteric Oghamists of the twentieth century. Two versions of his alphabet were given by Lewis Spence (1874–1955), in his book *The Mysteries of Britain* (1928), and, later, they formed the basis for the Ogham theories of Robert Graves (1895–1985). In his highly influential book *The White Goddess: A Historical Grammar of Poetic Myth*, Graves followed O'Flaherty's interpretations while conserving the older names of the Oghams.*

In 1977, Colin Murray (1942–1986), the leader of the Druidic organization called the Golden Section Order, published literature on

---

*Graves's book was first published in 1948, with a final revised and enlarged edition appearing in 1961 (American edition 1966). It was a seminal work for many later Pagan groups, including various religious Druid orders and "1734 Traditional Witchcraft," whose teachings on the "Roebuck in the Thicket" recall Graves's original 1944 forerunner text of *The White Goddess*. Pennick and Jackson's *The Celtic Oracle* (1992) also made reference to this Roebuck mythos.

the Oghams. It culminated in a divination-card deck produced in a limited edition of hand-colored cards. This handcraft technique followed Murray's periodical *The New Celtic Review*, which also featured hand-colored artwork. Along with the cards, Murray published a chart of correspondences that was heavily indebted to Graves's researches (1979). Murray called it "The Divine Game in the Essence—the sacred play with the planes of human and divine reality." At this time, in certain Druid and Pagan circles, Ogham was of great interst, being taught and discussed. Part of this milieu, and published in 1978, was Nigel Pennick's booklet titled *Ogham and Runic: Magical Writing of Old Britain and Northern Europe*. Also in that year appeared Eileen Hogan's *Ogham: Each Letter of the Alphabet is Presented with a Color and a Bird*. Tree Ogham, Bird Ogham, and Color Ogham, popularized by Robert Graves, remain the three most common forms.

Subsequently, after Colin Murray's tragic early death, his widow Liz published *The Celtic Tree Oracle* (Rider, 1988), which reworked the themes of the earlier Golden Section Order deck, but was color printed, not hand-colored. In 1992, Nigel Pennick and Nigel Jackson's *The Celtic Oracle: The Ancient Arts of the Druids* was published by Aquarian/Thorsons. It was a boxed set with twenty-five cards designed by Nigel Jackson.* By then, the Oghams had been absorbed fully into contemporary esoteric and Pagan usages, and in the early twenty-first century, numerous Ogham card decks are available.

For the record, it is important to determine as accurately as possible the earliest meanings of the Oghams.† But even when they have been determined as well as is humanly possible in the circumstances, this knowledge does not negate necessarily the value of later developments.

---

*The cards, although based on the tree system, also had tarot-like symbolic figures, such as The Queen of the West for *Eadha*, the Lapwing for *Ailim*, and The Hawk of May for *Saille*.

†The best scholarly source in this regard is Damian McManus's *A Guide to Ogam* (1991).

Devotees of religions often claim that the older a system is, then the closer it is to the "original," which is thus assumed to be the best and most pure form. This is the essence of all fundamentalisms. However, the nature of existence is change. Everything must evolve from age to age, keeping itself in harmony with the times. Otherwise, it will become progressively less useful as time passes, eventually becoming obsolete, and finally passing from being altogether. When we study the past, we must always bear in mind that it is the repository of errors as well as truths, and that, inevitably, new insights have arisen since any system was first organized. They must be accommodated if the system is to remain useful today and in the foreseeable future.

2

Meanings of the Ogham Feadha

TYPES AND ORDER OF OGHAM

Ogham is sometimes called the Celtic Tree Alphabet. This is because the basic meanings of the feadha (characters) correspond with certain trees. They are listed in several traditional texts, including the *Book of Ballymote* (1391) and O'Flaherty's *Ogygia* (1793). Similarly, the Gaelic *aibítir* (alphabet) has characters that correspond with trees, and the Welsh *Coelbren* is deeply connected with wood lore. Although there is a generally accepted Ogham correspondence system, there are numerous variations in recorded historic tree-correspondences for the feadha. The *Auraicept na n-Éces* tells of the different interpretations taught by autonomous colleges and independent Bards, so it is not a coherent system, having been standardized only in the twentieth century. Thus, the *Book of Ballymote* lists no fewer than 150 types of Ogham.

The standard or basic form of Ogham is *Ogham Craobh*, so called because the feadha resemble the branches of trees. Its English name is "Branch Ogham." It is designed to be cut into a hard material using a burin. Some of the other 149 types are variants of form, with different arrangements of strokes (*flesca*). There are Oghams named after things, such as *Rígh Ogam*, where each fidh is the name of a king (Old Irish *rí*);

Muc Ogam, where each has a corresponding color; *En Ogam*, where each is named after one of the ancient bird-names; and *Din Ogam*, "Hill Ogham," in which each fidh is called after terms connected with a hill. There are also cryptic Oghams, such as *Ogam Inarbach*, the "Ogham of Banishment"; *Taeb Ogham Tlachtga*, the "Side Ogham of Tlachtga"; and *Snaiti Snimach*, the "Twining, or Tangled Thread." These and others are described below.

The standard order of Ogham is: B, L, F, S, N; H, D, T, C, Q; M, G, Ng, St, R; A, O, U, E, I; Ea, Oi, Ui, Io, Æ. Some texts call the whole row of Branch Ogham "Be(i)th–Luis–Nion" (B, L, N), which are the first two and the last feadha of the first *aicme* (group of Ogham characters).

The letter order given in the *Book of Ballymote* is as in the list above. It begins with the feadha B, L, F. Certain commentators have suggested that the B, L, N order is the older form, and have applied it to their esoteric systems. The idea appears to come from an eighteenth-century antiquary, Edward Ledwich. In his *Antiquities of Ireland* (1792), he states that B, L, N was an early form. But elsewhere Ledwich contradicts himself, writing: "N was anciently the fifth letter" (Ledwich 1804, 338). R. A. S. Macalister, in his book *The Secret Languages of Ireland*, also states that for some time after its first appearance, the first three letters were B, L, N (1937, 27).

Ogham Terminology

Ogham has its own terminology, from the Irish. The word *Ogham* itself means an inscription written or engraved in the characters ascribed to the legendary Ogma Grianainech, though he may be an explanatory myth based on the name of the writing. Characters in Ogham are located with relation to a principal stem line or ridge, the *druim*, "back" or "ridge." In the earliest Ogham inscriptions on stone, this was actually the corner or edge arris at the junction of two flat surfaces. This druim stem is not a character in its own right, but only a guide. Its upper side is termed the left, and the underside, the right.

The individual lines composing the letters are drawn under, over, or through the druim. When the Oghams are cut on a squared stone or stick, then they are cut across the corner angle, which is thus the druim. In Scholastic Ogham, a druim is drawn as a straight line on which the lines are made. The word for one of these cuts or strokes is Old Irish *flesc* (pl. *flesca*), Scots Gaelic *fleasg*. This denotes a "line" or "stroke"; a "twig," "rod," "stave," or "wand"; a "wattle" or "lath"; with the additional meanings of "hoop," "band," "garland," and "rim (of a wheel)." A line of Ogham characters written along a druim is called *craobh*, a "bough" or "branch." Each Ogham "letter"—that is, the Ogham equivalent of a letter in an alphabet—is called *fidh* (or *fid*), a "tree," plural *feadha* (or *feda*). A fidh consists of one to five strokes. Each of the feadha is related to a specific tree, and so Ogham is sometimes called the Tree Alphabet. The whole Ogham alphabet together is called *An Ogam Craobh*, "The Ogham Branch."

Each of the five groups of Ogham characters is called an *aicme* (pl. *aicmí*), "rubric," "group," "class," or "denomination." The first three aicmí contain consonants; the fourth aicme is composed of vowels; while the final is of diphthongs. The first aicme, beginning with *Beith* (B, L, F, S, N) is drawn with one to five strokes at right angles below (right of) the druim. The second aicme, that of *Huath* (H, D, T, C, Q), is written with one to five strokes at right angles above (left of) the druim. The third aicme, of *Muin* (M, G, Ng, St, R), is made from one to five long strokes cut at an angle across the druim. The fourth aicme, *Ailm* (A, O, U, E, I), is made of one to five dots or short strokes cutting the druim at right angles. The feadha of the fifth aicme are known as *forfeadha*, "overtrees." These "overtrees" may have a later origin than the previous four aicmí, perhaps stemming from the Scholastic Oghams of the medieval monastic scriptoria.* They are composed of more complex strokes. Only the first two forfeadha are known from stone

---

*A *scriptorium* (pl. *scriptoria*) was a writing room in a monastery where manuscripts were copied by hand.

An Ogham Craobh, the standard "Tree-branch Ogham"
characters, showing *druim* (ridge), *flesc* (stroke), *fidh* (character),
and *aicme* (group).

inscriptions. *Eabhadh* (Ea) appears in several Irish inscriptions and in Britain at Crickhowell in Wales. *Oir* is known from the Bressay Stone from Cullingsburgh, Shetland.

Traditionally, since at least the time of the "Primary Bard of Britain," Taliesin (ca. 520–570 CE), Celtic Bards of the British Isles have used wood-related metaphors for poetry, and later referred to themselves by the kenning "carpenters of song" (Suggett 2006–2007, 251–52; Davies 1995). In a poem that refers both to the use of memory and of script (perhaps Ogham), Taliesin states:

> *I am the depository of song; I am a literary man;*
> *I love the high trees, that afford a protection above*
> *And a bard that composes, without earning anger.*
> (SKENE 1868, 1:524)

MacLonan, the chief poet of Ireland who died in the year 918 CE, appears to make a similar arboreal literary collocation:

> *Cormac of Cashel with his champions,*
> *Munster is his, may he long enjoy it;*
> *Around the King of Raith Bicli are cultivated,*
> *The letters and the trees.*
> (ATKINSON 1874, 205)

Because *An Ogam Craobh*, "The Ogham Branch," means the whole "alphabet," by analogy, it can also mean a complete knowledge of all aspects of Ogham, which includes poetry and literature. The Bardic Silver and Golden Branches, carried as emblems of office in ancient Ireland, refer to this high level of learning and creativity. In the *Immacallam in dá Thuarad* (Colloquy of the Two Sages) we are told:

Thus then went the youth [Néde] with a silvern branch above him; for this is what used to be above the *anruths* [Old Irish *ánrad*, poet

of the second order]: a branch of gold above the ollaves [Old Irish
ollam, chief poet]: a branch of copper over the rest of the poets.
(Stokes 1905, 11, 13)

In appearance, the Oghams are related to the Scandinavian
runic code called *kvistrúnar*, "twig-runes" or "branch-runes." It
appears that this variety of runic encryption came later than the
main use of Ogham for memorials, which was between the fourth
and eighth centuries CE. It is possible that the Ogham principle was
taken up by Scandinavian runemasters living in Ireland, the Isles,
or Northumbria, and applied by them to the runes.* Cryptic runes
and possible Oghams exist on a fragment of stone cross kept in the
church at Hackness, near Scarborough, Yorkshire. *Kvistrúnar* usually
encode letters as strokes on either side of an upright stave. The numbers of strokes refer to the number designated to a specific rune in a
prearranged sequence.

Ceart Ogam (the "Right Ogham") is the Ogham alphabet in
the original arrangement ascribed to Ogma; all other versions
are said to be variants of this original. In this work, I follow the
Book of Ballymote. The ascriptions are not all certain. Many of the
tree names are old forms or "obsolete" Irish. These were interpreted in
the nineteenth century by John O'Donovan. This uncertainty has also
given rise to variations in contemporary interpretation. The variations
are described in the appropriate sections below. A description of the
meaning of the individual *feadha* follows.

---

*A stone from Kilalloe, County Clare, Ireland, is rare in that it bears an inscription in
both Ogham and Norse runes carved by a runemaster named Thorgrimr who signed
the stone in Irish and Old Norse. The Ogham inscriptions reads BEANDACHT (AR)
TOROQR(IM), "A blessing on Thorgrimr," and the runic one states: (Th)urgrim risti
(k)rusina, "Thorgrimr carved this cross."

"Hear the voice of the Bard! Who Present, Past, & Future sees. Whose ears have heard, the Holy Word, That walk'd among the ancient trees."— William Blake, *Songs of Experience* (1794).

AN OGHAM CRAOBH—THE BRANCH OGHAM*

The First Aicme

Beith

The first tree of *An Ogam Craobh* is *Beth*, which in modern Irish is *beith* (Welsh *bedw*). This is the Birch tree (*Betula pendula*). Its phonetic equivalent is "B." The Birch is the the white tree of purification. According to the *Book of Ballymote* and the *Auraicept na n-Éces*, wood from a Birch tree was the substrate upon which the first Ogham word was inscribed. Samuel Taylor Coleridge wrote of the Birch as the "Lady of the Woods." The Birch is a pioneer tree, believed to be the first species of tree to recolonize the treeless wastes when the glaciers receded from the British Isles. Birch is a tree of emergence, for each spring it is the first deciduous woodland tree to put out leaves. Accordingly, it is classed as the first Peasant or Kiln Tree, with the corresponding color *ban*, "white." In traditional medicine, Birch is an analgesic, used as "teething twigs" for babies to chew. As an infusion, Birch tea, it was used in former times to treat kidney stones.

In Scotland, Birch is one of the nine woods used for kindling the ritual Need-Fire (Scots Gaelic *tein'-éigin*) of Beltane (*Là Bealltainn*) or the *samhnag* ("halloween bonfire") of Samhain. This is noted in a Scottish text in the collection of folkloric material known as the *Carmina Gadelica* that tells us to "Choose the birch of the waterfalls" (McNeill 1989, 84). Birching was used until well into the twentieth century on inmates of British and Manx prisons as corporal punishment. Anciently, it was a means of exorcising evil. Similarly, Birch twigs

---

*The spellings of the Ogham names given here reflect how they appear in some older sources. However, as the orthography of medieval Old Irish was inconsistent, variant spellings often exist for each name. In Damian McManus's *A Guide to Ogam*, the names from the manuscript tradition are given in standardized Old Irish form as follows (1991, 3): *Beithe, Luis, Fern, Sail, Nin, hÚath, Dair, Tinne, Coll, Cert, Muin, Gort, (n)Gétal, Straif, Ruis, Ailm, Onn, Úr, Edad, Idad, Ébad, Ór, Uilen, Pín/Iphín*, and *Emancholl*. Importantly, McManus also presents philological evidence for the original letter-name meanings in the earliest version of the alphabet (1991, 36–39).

form part of the traditional besom, used for sweeping away dirt and bad luck (see chap. 5).

Hats made of birchbark are a sign of the dead. One was found on the remains of the Celtic lord excavated from a sixth-century BCE burial mound at Hochdorf near Stuttgart in south Germany. It was a circular, flattened cone. This is paralleled by the words of an English ballad from more than two thousand years later, "The Wife of Usher's Well," which refers to the birchen hats of the wife's three dead sons, when they reappear as ghosts. Whether the Birch specifically relates to the Celtic doctrine of transmigration of souls, or is a sign of the purification of the dead, is unknown. The traditional material for babies' cradles is Birch wood.

The Birch is the tree of sexuality, par excellence. The Welsh Bard Dafydd ap Gwilym (ca. 1315/1320–ca. 1350/1370)—one of whose lovers, Morfudd ("Goddaughter of May"), was a married woman—wrote a poem in which he attempts to convince a nun to come away with him:

> *Is it true, the girl that I love,*
> *That you do not desire birch, the strong growth of*
> *   summer?*
> *Be not a nun in spring,*
> *Asceticism is not as good as a bush.*
> *As for the warrant of ring and habit,*
> *A green dress would ordain better.*
> *Come to the spreading birch,*
> *To the religion of the trees and the cuckoo.*
> (REES AND REES 1967, 287)

In contemporary Ogham lore, the Birch-fidh serves to protect against all harm, physical and spiritual. It allows us to deal with bad things; to clear them away, so that a new beginning can take place, unhindered by "unfinished business."

Luis

The second Ogham fidh is called *Luis*, whose tree is the Rowan or Quickbeam (*Sorbus acuparia*). *Luis* is an "obsolete" feminine Irish name for the tree, which is called *caorthann* in modern Irish. In Welsh, it is called *criafol*. The gloss on *Luis* in the *Book of Ballymote* is *Leam*, meaning "Elm."

The Rowan is a tree of hedgerows and woodland and is the second Peasant or Kiln Tree (but Elm is a Royal or Chieftain Tree). The *Book of Ballymote* describes the poetic name of Luis as "*Li súla*, delight of the eye, that is *luis*" (Calder 1917, 277). This color is "flame," the modern Irish *luisne*, a "red glare" (with an inner light, like fire), is used to describe the first light of dawn, with the additional meaning of a "sheen" or "luster." Another color correspondence is *liath*, "gray," the mixing of light and darkness.

Rowan is a powerful tree of protection, whose presence at a location suppresses all psychic harm. It is the tutelary tree or "plant badge" of the Scottish clans MacCallum, MacLachlan, Malcolm, and Menzies. In his *Flora Scotica*, John Lightfoot noted that Rowans were plentiful in the vicinity of stone circles in Scotland. Rowans are planted outside the front door of houses to ward off bad luck, baneful magic, and autonomous evil (Lightfoot 1777, I:257). The defensive powers of Rowan are recounted in the traditional Scottish rhyme:

> *Rowan tree and red threid*
> *Gar the witches tyne their speed.*

Translated into standard English, this is: "Rowan tree and red thread make the witches lose their speed." Magically, Rowan is effective against the "wrath and anger of all men." As a magical protection, Scotswomen traditionally make necklaces out of Rowan berries, strung together on red linen thread.

In the counties on the Anglo-Welsh border, it is customary to make crosses of Birch and Rowan twigs, tied with red thread. They are placed over doors on May morning and left in place until the next May Day. In Scotland, Rowan rods are used in the same way. In horse-drawn days, Rowan was used for the horsemen's switches or whips used to subdue "bewitched" horses. Rods of Rowan were used in rhabdomancy for finding metals hidden beneath the earth. Festal cakes or bannocks baked over a fire of Rowan wood are considered to have apotropaic powers.

Mythologically, Rowan brings magical transformation. The Irish tale of "The Wooing of Étaín" tells how Queen Fúamnach, wife of the underworldly Midir, hits Étaín with a Rowan rod. Immediately, Étaín is transformed into a pool of water, then a worm and a fly that generates a heavenly fragrance and sweet music.

In contemporary usage, *Luis* serves to protect its user against psychic attack. It is an aid for the development of the power of second sight, and self-control against inner anger. In a divination, *Luis* warns that the subject is under external psychic stress, with the proviso that if he or she takes the appropriate precautions, then there will be no harm.

Fearn

The third Ogham fidh is *Fearn*, "F." *Fearn* corresponds with the Alder tree (*Alnus glutinosa*). In modern Irish, Alder is called *fearnóg* (Welsh *gwernen*). *Fern* also means a "shield" and the "mast of a ship." It is related to the word *fearsaid*, which can mean a "shaft," "spindle," or the "ulna bone." As "shaft," it refers to the Alder piles which were used all over Europe for the foundations of buildings in wetlands. Alder wood is the best timber for this purpose. The foundations of wetland cities such as Venice and Rotterdam, lowland cathedrals like Winchester, watermills, lake villages, and the island crannogs of the British Isles were built upon piles of Alder. Symbolically, *Fearn* is a tree of fire used to free the earth from water. On a human scale, protection against the wet ground comes in the shape of Alder-wood clogs for the feet. It also provides the wood used in making the "magic whistles" used to "whistle up the wind."

In traditional crafts, Alder wood was used for making milk pails and other containers used in the dairy. The *Word Ogham* of

Crannogs, lake villages, and cities like Rotterdam were built on the resistant piles of the Alder tree (Ogham *Fearn*).

Mac ind Óic gives *Fearn*'s kenning as "guarding of milk" (Calder 1917, 285). Although *Fearn* has the interpretation "shield" and is described as "good for shields" in the *Book of Ballymote* (Atkinson 1874, 209), it seems that in ancient times Alder was used as a second-best alternative to wood from the Linden (Lime) tree. According to ancient chronicles and sagas, both the Anglo-Saxon and Scandinavian warriors favored shields made from Limewood, covered with leather.

In the smithy, this tree of fire was an essential part of sword-making. Sword-smiths prized Alder wood because it furnished the best charcoal for forging. In later times, its military connection was continued with the new technology of gunpowder production, for Alder charcoal was the best ingredient. The Old Irish "Song of the Forest Trees" in the text known as *Aidedh Ferghusa meic Léide* (The Death of Fergus) describes Alder as "The very battle-witch of all woods, the tree that is hottest in the fight" (O'Grady 1892, 178). In contemporary usages, *Fearn* is best used for personal protection in conflicts, and for freeing oneself from magical bindings of every kind.

The fidh *Fearn* is associated with the color called *flann*, "blood-red" or "crimson." This is because when an Alder tree is cut down, its sap turns red like blood. Like the Yew, the Alder is seen as a "bleeding tree," and so, in traditional belief, to fell an Alder tree is a sacrilege that will bring retribution in the form of the transgressor being burnt out of house and home. In traditional crafts, the Alder provides fabric dyes. Three dyes can be prepared from the Alder tree: the bark makes red; the twigs make brown; and the flowers make green. These *Fearn* dyes were the basic colors for the ancient plaid patterns that evolved into the Scottish tartans of the present day.

In British mythology, the Alder tree is connected with King Bran, whose mummified oracular head was carried around Britain. Finally, his followers buried it at Bryn Gwyn, the White Mount of Trinovantium, now occupied by the Norman White Tower of the Tower of London. There, until it was dug up by King Arthur, it served as the magical shield of Britain against her enemies. According to Robert Graves in

The White Goddess, the "singing head" of Bran symbolizes the "head" of the Alder tree, the topmost branch (1966, 170). This "head" is visible in winter when the tree had lost its leaves. Then the Alder's black cones and unopened catkins give the tree a dense, purple-tinged crown.

Saille

Saille, phonetically "S," corresponds with the Sally tree (White Willow, *Salix alba*). In the old Irish Brehon Law, the name for this tree is given as *sail*, and in modern Irish, *sailech* (in Welsh, it is *helygen*). The Sally tree is the third of the Peasant or Kiln Trees. Its corresponding color in *Muc Ogham* is *sodath*, interpreted as "bright" or "fine." The Sally Tree loves water and grows close to pools, streams, and rivers.

In traditional medicine, the bark of the Sally tree provided relief from the disorders and diseases of dampness, such as headache, the ague, rheumatism, and arthritis. Its young osiers are pliant, finding many uses in basket-, wattle- and hurdle-making. It is used as a binding-material in thatched roofs; in wattle-and-daub walling, and also as the withies used to bind the Birch twigs onto the broomstick of traditional besoms. When the Welsh "wood-alphabet" called *Coelbren y Beirdd* was allegedly revived during King Henry IV's persecution of Welsh culture after 1400, it was said to be the basketmakers who were the keepers of the tradition.*

As well as being pliant when young, Willow is a resonant wood when mature. In traditional craft, the Willow provides the material for the sound box of the *cláirseach* (Irish Harp) and the blades of English cricket bats. It is one of the nine woods used in the Scottish Need-Fire (*tein'-éigin*) and the bonfires of May and November, though the Old Irish "Song of the Forest Trees" tells us: "The noble willow burn not, a tree sacred to poems" (O'Grady 1892, 178).

---

*As there is no recorded historical evidence for this symbolic story, or for the Bardic alphabet (which is treated in chap. 6), it is probably a nationalist tale originating in the nineteeth-century Celtic Revival.

In contemporary Ogham lore, *Saille* is a fidh of being pliant: the flowing, watery symbolism of coming into harmony naturally with the flow of events, most notably the phases of the Moon. In divination, its power is greater in darkness than in daylight, except when the Moon is visible during the day. Its power fluctuates with the cycle of the Moon's phases.

Nin

Nin, *Nuin*, or *Nion* is the last letter of the first aicme. It has the phonetic value of "N," and corresponds with the Ash tree (*Fraxinus excelsior*). "A check on peace is *nin*, namely ash, for of it are made the spear-shafts by which the peace is broken," as the *Book of Ballymote* tells us (Calder 1917, 91). The *Book of Ballymote* also has the gloss *nendait*, which may mean "Nettle," for *Nin*.

The Ash is the fourth Peasant or Kiln Tree. In the Brehon Laws, it is *Iundius*. In Old Irish it was *uinnius*, and its modern Irish name is *fuinseog*, and in Welsh *onnen*. The color associated with *Nion* is *necht*, "white," also "clean, pure." Ash is valued because it is fast growing, giving a hard-wearing wood better than any other European tree. The wood is heavy, strong, but with a certain elasticity. It takes a fine polish and bends well when seasoned. An Ash beam will take a heavier load, pro rata, than any other tree. In former times, Ash was the wood of choice for makers of military spear shafts, and it is still used for making the now illegal otter-spears. Magically, Ash is used in charming away warts.

Of Ash, the Old Irish "Song of the Forest Trees" tells us: "Dark is the colour of the ash: timber that makes the wheels to go; rods he furnishes for horsemen's hands, and his form turns battle into flight" (O'Grady 1892, 278).

According to contemporary insights, the Ash is the tree of rebirth, linking that which is above with that which is below: the worlds of the spirit and of matter. It is the passage between the inner world and the outer world. Symbolically, the bunches of fruits that resemble and are called "keys" signify the power to unlock future events. But, just as the seeds in these keys germinate only in the second year after falling to the ground, unlocking the future may not be instant.

The Second Aicme

Huath

The first fidh of the second aicme is *Huath*, sometimes rendered as *hUath* or *Uath*, with the phonetic value of "H." This phoneme is absent from Irish Gaeilge and Scots Gaelic; it is used only as an aspirant before an initial vowel, or in foreign loanwords for which there is no equivalent. It appears as *uath* in Cormac's *Glossary* (O'Donovan 1868, 165). Another meaning of *uath* is as a numeral substantive, meaning a "unit," anything single. In Ogham lore, *Huath* signifies the Whitethorn or Hawthorn tree (*Crataegus monogyna*), which the Book of Ballymote describes as "a crooked tree, or a bush, because of her thorns" (Atkinson 1874, 209). Brehon Law calls this tree *sceith*. In modern Irish, it is *sceach*, and in Welsh, *ysbyddaden* or *draenen wen*. A gloss in the *Book of Ballymote* gives *Rge* as an alternative name for this character.

The Hawthorn is the fifth Peasant or Kiln Tree whose color, *hUath*, "terrible," is interpreted in modern terms as purple. Another name for this thorn tree is the May tree, and *Huath* blossoms in the Merry Month of May. The blooming of the May tree was the marker of May Day and Beltane (Irish Gaeilge *Lá Bealtaine*; Scots Gaelic *Latha Bealltainn*), rather than a calendar date. This is remembered in the old English adage "Ne'er cast a clout, till May be out" (Do not cast off your winter clothes until you see a May tree blossom). Traditionally, it is unlucky to bring May blossom into the house.

Traditional craftsmen prized wood from the roots of Hawthorn for making combs and boxes, for the wood is fine-grained and takes a brilliant polish. Hawthorn wood burns with the hottest flame, and Hawthorn charcoal is reputed to give out more heat than that of other woods. An ancient meaning of *hUath* is "dreadful," "terrible," or "horrible," perhaps referring to its daunting, thorny nature. The *Auraicept na n-Éces* tells us: "A meet of hounds is *huath*, . . . or because it is formidable owing to its thorns" (Calder 1917, 91). This meaning of "thorn" is identical with the meaning of the Germanic rune called *Thurisaz* (Anglo-Saxon *Thorn* and Norse *Þurs*), which has a daunting, defensive quality.

In 1485, it was from a thorn bush at Bosworth Field that the crown from the helmet of the slain King Richard III was brought to the Welsh lord, Henry Tudor, who thus proclaimed himself King Henry VII of England and Wales. Subsequently, Henry VII's "plant badge" was the Hawthorn. In contemporary understanding, *Huath* is the Ogham fidh of protection against all ills, invoking the power of the Otherworld.

In Irish folk tradition, this tree is considered to be a "Gentle" or "Fairy" tree.* It brings extreme misfortune to anyone foolhardy enough to tamper with one. The death of one's children or livestock and the loss of all of one's money is the traditional fate of such an individual. The lore of Thorn trees is dealt with at length in chapter 5.

Duir

The fidh *Duir* corresponds with the Common or Pedunculate Oak (*Quercus robur*), which in modern Irish is called *dair* and in Welsh, *derwen*. It has the phonetic value of "D." *Duir* is the second Royal or Chieftain Tree (after Elm, the "gloss" of *Luis*). Its color is *dubh*, black. Throughout Europe, the Oak is considered to be the most powerful tree of all. The *Book of Ballymote* refers to it as "the oak of fate from the wood" (Atkinson 1874, 209). It is invariably the holy tree of the sky-god, called in different places Zeus, Jupiter, Taranis, Daronwy, the Dagda, Perun, Perkunas, Ziu, Thunor, and Thor.

The Oak was the holy tree of the Celtic Druids, and its name, *Duir*, is related to the Irish word *dúr*, "hard, unyielding, durable." The medieval Welsh poem "Cad Goddeu" (The Battle of the Trees) tells us of Oak:

> *The oak, quickly moving,*
> *Before him, tremble heaven and earth.*
> *A valiant door-keeper against an enemy,*
> *his name is considered.*
>
> (SKENE 1868, I:280)

---

*This usage is not to be confused with the epithet *gentle* as meaning "royal" or "chieftain."

Celtic holy wells are enhanced by the power of the Thorn and
other holy trees that grow alongside them.

Commentaries on *Dair* from early Irish laws refer to its size, use in woodworking, and valuable acorns (for fattening pigs).

The Oak is the "plant badge" of the Irish O'Connors and several Scottish clans, including Clan Buchanan, Cameron, Kennedy, and Stewart. It is the "crest badge" of the Andersons (MacAndrews) and Clan MacEwen (the House of Bardrochat), which shows a cut-off Oak trunk from which new sprouts are growing. The Cornish surname Derrick is from *derowek*, an "Oak grove."

The bird of this fidh is relevant to the king of all trees, for it is the wren (Irish *dreolan*), called the "king of all birds" though one of the smallest of all indigenous birds in Europe. It was a sacred bird of the Druids, and there was an ancient *geis* (taboo) against killing wrens. The geis continued in post-Pagan times, except on St. Stephen's Day (Boxing Day, December 26), when the Wren Boys hunted and killed a wren, and then paraded it around, singing the local Wren Boys' Song. The custom exists throughout the British Isles and Brittany, and, although wrens are no longer killed, the tradition is maintained, from the performance of "The Cutty Wren" in England to the *bodhrán*-playing Wren Boys of Ireland. The Wren Boys' Song from the Englishry of Pembrokeshire* begins with the invocation "Joy, health, love, and peace, be all here in this place," and goes on to tell of the difficulties involved in catching the wren: "We have traveled many miles, over hedges and stiles, in search of our king." In Welsh-speaking Denbighshire and Flintshire, the song "Hela'r Dryw" (Hunting the Wren) is sung, and, on the Isle of Man, "Shelg yn Drean" (Hunt the Wren!). The Irish version, sung in English, tells us:

> *The wren, the wren, the king of all birds,*
> *On Stephen's Day was caught in the Furze.*
> *Though he was little his honour was great,*

---

*The Englishry is part of Pembrokeshire settled by English and Flemish settlers after 1100, and consequently not Welsh-speaking. The landscape of the Englishry differs markedly from the Celtic landscapes outside it, and it is divided from it by a demarcation line called the Landsker.

So give us a penny to give us a treat!
Up with the kettle and down with the pan,
And give us a penny to bury the wren!

The wren is the "bird badge" of the Pennick family.

To the contemporary understanding, this important fidh signifies strength. Things of great strength are sometimes hidden from view, like the "Bog Oaks" buried beneath the peat in the bogs of Ireland and the Fens of East Anglia. But, once found, they can be recovered and be of great service. Spiritually, *Duir* may serve as a psychic doorway to inner experiences. *Duir* enables us to see the invisible and to become unseen; to allow entry of those who should enter and to exclude those who ought not. Further Oak lore can be found in chapters 4 and 5.

However, Roderic O'Flaherty, writing in the seventeeth century, stated that "*Duir*, vulgarly *Cuileann*," represented "the Scarlet Oak, Broom, Holm, Holly." Many historic Ogham ascriptions are contentious, and it was only in the twentieth century that they appear to have been standardized.

Tinne

With a phonetic value of "T," *Tinne*, *Tine*, or *Tindi* is given by the *Book of Ballymote* as corresponding with "holly [*tinne*] or elderberry [*trom*] in the forest" (Calder 1917, 277). Modern Oghamists usually associate it with the Holly (*Ilex aquifolium*). However, a gloss in the *Book of Ballymote* also associates Holly (*Quilleann*) with the fidh *Quert* (see below) (Calder 1917, 277).

Because of this multiple ascription, there is some confusion as to the meaning of *Tinne*. The Rowan tree is more commonly identified with *Luis* (*caorthann*). However, the modern Irish word for Holly is *cuileann*, cognate with the Welsh name, *celyn*. In the *Word Ogham* of Mac ind Óic, *smir guaili*, "fires of coal," is kenning for holly (Calder 1917, 285) and therefore *Tinne*; fire may also be related to Holly (and Rowan) by its fire-red berries. Holly wood does burn exceptionally well. In the Old

The Wren Boys make their annual ceremonial outing on St. Stephen's Day (Boxing Day, December 26), having traveled many miles, over hedges and stiles, in search of their "king" (inset).

Irish "Song of the Forest Trees" we are reminded: "Holly, burn it green; holly, burn it dry: of all trees whatsoever the critically best is holly" (O'Grady 1892, 278).

As fire and as Holly, the fidh has the meaning of "warmth," "shelter" and "protection" (against the elements). In the Middle Irish romance *Buile Suibhne* (The Frenzy of Suibhne), the Wild Man–like eponymous hermit gives Holly the kenning "little sheltering one . . . door against the wind" (O'Keefe 1913, 67). Holly sticks are used in the divinatory Irish children's Hallowe'en game called "Building the House," where twelve pairs of sticks are arranged in a circle, thrust into the ground, brought together at the top, and tied. The coupled twigs are named after the boys and girls present at the game. Then a burning turf is placed at the center of the circle, and the first pair of twigs that catch fire denotes which boy and girl will be the first to marry.

Holly is the tree most associated with the traditional British Yuletide festivities, being called Christ's Thorn in some northern dialects. It crowns Old Father Christmas, and appears in the ancient carol "The Holly and the Ivy," where its berries are "as red as any blood." In certain parts of Wales, Holly was used to draw blood in a Yuletide custom called "Holly Beating" or "Holming," which was observed on St. Stephen's Day (Boxing Day, December 26). In the nineteenth century, it was described in Tenby, Pembrokeshire, as "a furious onslaught being made by men and boys, armed with large bushes of the prickly holly, on the naked and unprotected arms of female domestics, and others of a like class" (Davies 1911, 61–62). This aspect of midwinter misrule was suppressed by the Tenby police in 1857, and by similar actions elsewhere. Perhaps related to Holly Beating is its part in the martial arts, where it is portrayed as the club of the Wild Man. Holly is the "plant badge" of several Scottish clans: Drummond, Macinnes, Mackenzie, and Macmillan. The "crest badge" of the Maxwells shows a stag standing in front of a Holly bush.

Traditional crafts use the hard, white wood of the Holly in several ways. The *Auraicept na n-Éces* tells how it was "one of the three timbers of the chariot-wheel" (Calder 1917, 91). Holly is good for the stocks of light driving-whips and walking sticks, as well as the cudgels and clubs employed by practitioners of the northern European martial arts. Crooked branches of Holly were used as "crook sticks" for suspending the cauldron over the fire. A strong wood, Holly can withstand both the heat of the fire and the load of the cauldron and its contents without breaking. In former times, small clinker-built Irish fishing boats had keels made of Holly wood because it wears smooth and slides well on gravel beaches. In preindustrial days, Holly printing-blocks were used to print fabrics.

In contemporary usage, *Tinne* is a fidh of unification, employed for personal might and main, used in a balanced manner. It has a strong male element, which is connected specifically with fatherhood and posterity.

Coll

The fourth Ogham fidh of the second aicme is *Coll*, with the phonetic value of "K" or a hard "C." It signifies the "Hazel of the wood" (*Corylus avellana*), the third Royal or Chieftain Tree. Its ancient name is the same in modern Irish, while in Welsh it is *collen*. The *Auraicept na n-Éces* tells us that in Morann mac Máin's *Word Ogham*, Hazel is "*cainiu fedaib*, the fairest of trees," and in Mac ind Óic's *Word Ogham*, it is "*cara bloisc*, the friend of cracking"—presumably from its nuts, known sometimes as filberts (Calder 1917, 279, 287). Brehon Law glosses *Coll* for its nuts and its wattles and also numbers it among the Chieftain Trees (Joyce 1903, 2:287). According to country lore, the Hazel first produces nuts only after nine years' growth. Hazel is a tree of knowledge. According to Irish myth, over Connla's Well, in County Tipperary, grew the nine Hazels of wisdom and inspiration, the Hazels of the science of poetry, "out of which were obtained the feats of the sages" (Rhŷs 1901, 1:392). The Heralds of ancient Ireland carried white Hazel wands as symbols of office, representing their ability to use words and giving them free passage as noncombatants. At royal inaugurations in Ireland, the *filid* (Bards) gave the king a wand of Hazel as a sign of his accession.

More recently, in Wales, the white Hazel was involved in the hurtful custom of sending the *ffon wen* ("white stick") anonymously to a rejected lover. This revelation of the truth would take place on or near the wedding-day of his or her former partner. The ffon wen was a freshly peeled Hazel stick, sometimes trimmed with a black ribbon bow, and accompanied by insulting rhymes. In later years, they were sent by the Royal Mail. The custom continued longest in western Montgomeryshire.

According to *Silva Gadelica* and Eleanor Hull's *Folklore of the British Isles* (1928), many British and Irish sacred places were originally Hazel groves. In the early medieval period in Scandinavia, Hazel poles were used to delimit the ritual enclosure known as the *völlr haslaðr*, "enhazeled field." In Norse terminology, these round-headed poles were called *höslur*, "hazles," or *tiösnur*. Once a field had been enhazeled, then the formal rules of battle applied there. Both in the single combat called *holmganga* and in full-scale formal battles between armies, the "theater of conflict" was cut off from the normal world of everyday life by Hazel posts, which formed a boundary around it. The modern boxing ring and all rectangular sports fields such as those used for Association football (soccer), rugby, and American football are descendants of the "enhazeled field" by way of the *lists* (enclosed fields of combat) of the medieval tournament.

Hazel is a tree whose wood can be used magically. The late medieval *Book of Saint Albans* (1486) records a magical technique for invisibility that employs a Hazel rod one and a half fathoms in length (nine English feet; 2.74 meters). A green Hazel twig is implanted in its end. Another magic Hazel implement is recalled in the Irish legend of "The Ancient Dripping Hazel." In this story, a certain magic Hazel tree dripped venom. Fionn mac Cumhaill cut down the tree and made it into a shield that emitted poisonous gases and killed his enemies. "Fionn's shield" is a poetic kenning for magical protection by a diagram containing all of the feadha of Ogham. It also means a satirical poem that carries a curse upon the subject of the satire.

In his *Itinerary and Description of Wales* (1193), Giraldus Cambrensis wrote how Welsh people kept their teeth spotlessly clean with Hazel twigs (Rhys 1912, 171), and forked Hazel twigs were used by rhabdomants in water divining. Here, the Hazel was another means of "finding out." In ancient Ireland, the intoxicating drink of Hazel mead was prized for its qualities. In Scotland, the "plant badge" of the Colquhouns is the Hazel, and the Cornish surnames Collett and Collick refer to Hazel trees.

The contemporary interpretation of *Coll* is as a fidh of clear perception and inspired consciousness.

Quert

The final fidh of the second aicme is contentious. Standing for "Q" is *Quert*, or *Queirt*, generally taken to mean the Crab Apple tree (*Malus sylvestris*). An obsolete term for an Apple tree in Scots Gaelic was *cuirt*; this was replaced by *abhall*, which is akin to Irish Gaeilge *abhaill* and Welsh *afallen*. It is the seventh Kiln or Peasant Tree of the Ogham Craobh. However, the *Book of Ballymote* also gives two alternative ascriptions for Quert: Aspen and Rowan, while a gloss in another section ascribes Q as *quilleann*, Holly. *Quert*'s color is given variously as "apple-green" and *quiar*, "mouse-colored" (Calder 1917, 291).

Legends from various parts of Europe show that the apple is symbolic of eternal life. The Greek tradition tells of the Golden Apples of the Hesperides, the Norse speaks of the goddess Iduna and the apples of immortality, while Celtic tradition has the Isle of Avalon, to which King Arthur is taken after his last battle, to heal his wounds. Perhaps to symbolize the afterlife, at the funeral of Velters Cornewall of Moccas in Herefordshire, April 1768, twelve women walked in the funeral cortege carrying Apple-tree branches.

Symbolically, the five strokes to the left of the stem of the Ogham fidh can be seen as reflecting the fivefold petals of the Apple flower, and the five receptacles for the seeds within the fruit itself. Unlike the cultivated species of Apple, the Crab Apple is a thorn-bearing tree, giving *Quert* protective qualities. The Crab Apple is the "plant badge" of the Scots Clan Lamont.

The Third Aicme

Muin

Muin or *Min* has a phonetic value of "M," and is usually ascribed to the "vine-tree" (Grapevine, Lat. *vitis*), which the *Book of Ballymote* associates with *midiu*, "mead," presumably drawing a connection to wine made from the grapevine (Calder 1917, 277). O'Flaherty's *Ogygia* gives "Muin, vulgarly *Fineamhuin*, the Vine tree." However, in modern Irish, the Grapevine is *finúin*. This plant is not indigenous to the British Isles, but it was grown in climatically favorable parts of Britain during the Roman occupation, and wine plays an integral part in Christian ritual.

Muin is the fourth Royal or Chieftain Tree. However, in the Irish language, *muine* has the meaning of a "thicket" of any thorny plant, so the correlation of this Ogham with the Grapevine may not be so strong. Its corresponding color is Old Irish *mbracht*, "variegated" (Calder 1917, 291). According to contemporary interpretation, *Muin* denotes the ability to range over a wide area and gather together everything we need. Once gathered together, they are assimilated into us, aiding our inner development.

Gort

The fidh *Gort* has the phonetic value of "G." It represents the Ivy (*Hedera helix*). It is the fifth Royal Tree. Ivy is *eidhneán* in modern Irish; in Welsh, the name of this "tree" is *eiddew*. But the meaning of this fidh is problematical, for the Irish word *gort* means a "tilled field," not Ivy. Also, a gloss in the *Book of Ballymote* gives the word *gius*, meaning "cornfield" (Calder 1917, 277). *Gorm*, "blue," is the color associated with *Gort*. Ivy is the "plant badge" of the Gordon clan.

According to contemporary interpretation, *Gort* represents the changes that are necessary for growth, and the requirement that all

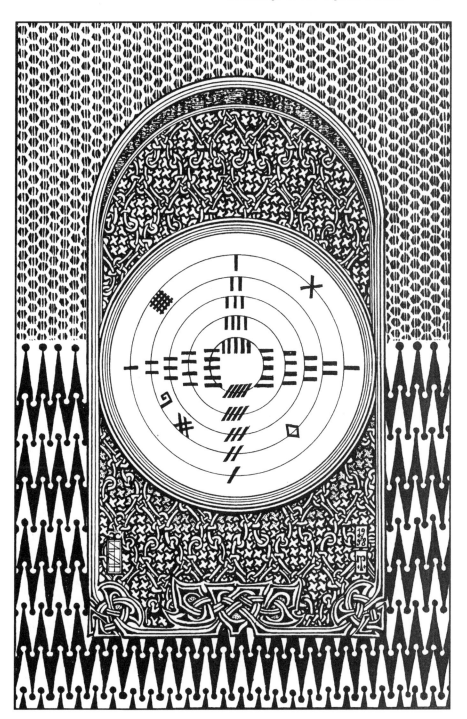

Fionn's Shield

things be related to the Earth. Just as it is necessary to till the fields in order to reap a harvest later, so it is necessary to do the "groundwork" in anything before we can reap the benefits. Although the Ivy uses other plants or walls for support, to survive, it must remain rooted in the ground. Beginning as a small, weak, herblike plant, it grows slowly over many years to become an enormously thick, woody, serpentine tree in its own right.

Ngetal

The thirteenth fidh is *Ngetal* or *Ngedal*, "Ng," *Getal*, the Reed. In Irish its modern name is *giolcach*, and in Welsh, *cawnen*.

The Reed is the first of the Kiln or Shrub trees. Its color is *nglas*, "green," usually thought of as a yellowish green (Calder 1917, 291). A *Book of Ballymote* gloss gives *gilcach*, "broom," for this fidh (Calder 1917, 91, 93, 277).

It may appear strange that the Irish Bards called the Reed a tree, but the contemporary definition of what is and what is not a tree is a relatively recent scientific convention. In traditional perception and language, different criteria prevail. The most obvious example is the many kinds of "fish" described by the English language that are not classified as fish (*Pisces*) at all by scientific taxonomists: shellfish, jellyfish, crayfish, and whalefish. According to traditional definitions, any plant with woody stems, such as a Reed or Ivy, is a tree. It seems that in ancient times, the Irish scribes classified the Reed as a tree because its hard, resistant stems make good pens.*

Ngetal is a preserver: as a pen, the Reed preserves memory and knowledge; as a rod, it preserves measure; and as roofing, it preserves the house. The traditional use of the Reed is as a covering—for weatherproofing the roof of the house with Reed thatch, and, as a floor-covering, especially in winter, when Reeds served as insulation. As a

---

*According to the romantic history recounted in Iolo Morganwg's *Barddas* (see chap. 6), the Welsh scribes' favorite material, *plagawd*, was also made from reeds.

Bardic tree, however, *Ngetal* is the fidh of written communication, thereby maintaining human culture over time.

The many uses of the Reed in traditional society are reflected in its contemporary symbolic meanings. In addition to signifying preservation, *Ngetal* denotes the flexibility that we must possess if we are to survive in the prevailing circumstances without sacrificing our integrity. From its use in thatching, and as the covert in which birds take refuge, it is the container and protector of living things, just as writing is the container and protector of thought and culture.

Straif

The fourteenth fidh is called *Straif* or *Straiph*. With the phonetic equivalent "St" (or "Z"), it signifies the Blackthorn or Sloe tree, *Prunus spinosa*, which is counted as the sixth Royal Tree. Its Old Irish name was *droigion* (*draidean* in Brehon Law, modernly, *draghan* or *draighean*), and in Welsh, it is *draenen*. *Straif*'s corresponding color is *srorca* or *sorcha*, "bright-colored." Blackthorn is a tree of power, whose name has the connotations of "punishment" and "strife." Staves made from its wood, carried by witches, warlocks, and wizards, have always been renowned for their magical power.

Physically, the Sloe tree has a very hard and durable wood, excellent for making walking sticks, shillelaghs, cudgels, and the "Black Rod" of wizards. It is a fine plant for forming hedges, with formidable thorns that make an impenetrable barrier. Blackthorn produces suckers, which, as the years pass, grow to make a single plant the nucleus of an impenetrable thorny thicket. Medicinally, the fruit of the Blackthorn is the key component in sloe gin.

The contemporary view of *Straif* in magic and divination sees it as a provider of power on both the material and nonmaterial levels. Straif gives strength and determination to the willpower: it contains the strength we need to resist and defeat adversity, and to control or ward off magical attack. Thus, it is considered the most powerful fidh for overthrowing all resistance to one's will.

According to contemporary Bardo-Druidic teachings, *nwyvre*, symbolized by the wyvern, a two-legged dragon, is the underlying subtle quality that empowers existence.

Ruis

Ruis, with the phonetic value of "R," corresponds with the Elder tree or Bourtree (*Sambucus nigra*). In the Brehon Law and in modern Irish, this is *trom* and in Welsh *ysgawen*).

The bark and flowers of the Elder possess healing properties, but the vapors that accumulate in Elder woodland are reputed to produce disease and even bring death to those who might linger there for too long. Perhaps it is significant that Walter Tyrell, the archer who killed the Norman King, William II Rufus, shot him from beneath an Elder tree. The color ascribed to *Ruis* is *ruadh*, one of the many forms of red recognized in prescientific days. The Cornish surnames Scawn and Scown refer to the Elder Tree, which is *scawen* in the Cornish tongue.

In certain parts of the British Isles, it is considered extremely inauspicious to burn Elder wood in a house. Flowering branches of Elder, however, are effective in warding off flies from byres and stables. As a tree of magic in Ireland, Elder sticks were reputed to have been the steeds of witches in place of the more common besoms or hurdles. The Elder is the origin of two medicinal alcoholic beverages which ward off the cold and illness: elderflower wine, brewed in June and July from the creamy-white flowers, and elderberry wine, fermented from the purple-black fruits that ripen in August and September.

According to contemporary sensibilities, *Ruis* signifies the three aspects of time present in the Three Fates. As the Weird Sisters, they represent the ever-present threefold aspects of existence: beginning, middle, and end. *Ruis* denotes the acceptance all three aspects that we must have if we are to lead balanced lives. *Ruis* is thus a fidh of timelessness, expressed as the unity of all time.

The Fourth Aicme

Ailm

Ailm, the Elm Tree (*Ulmus minor*), is the first fidh of the fourth aicme. It is the first Royal or Chieftain Tree in the *Book of Ballymote*. *Ailm* has the phonetic value of "A." The kind of Elm represented by this Ogham fidh is the Western variety known commonly as the "Cornish Elm" (*Ulmus minor* var. *stricta*). Before the 1970s, when Elms in the British Isles were devastated by Dutch Elm Disease, this variety was common in Cornwall, Devon, and southwestern Ireland. Unlike most Elms, this is a wayside tree that does not grow in woodland. This fidh appears in the name of the letter (*litir*) "a" in the obsolete Scots Gaelic alphabet: *ailm*, "Elm." Brehon Law calls Elm *leam*.

The ascription of *Ailm* to Elm is not always used by Oghamists, however, because in the "obsolete" Irish of the *Book of Ballymote*, the correspondence has been interpreted as a "fir tree." Brehon Law reckons fir/ pine as one of the seven Chieftain Trees, calling it *ochtach*, "wood . . . used in making puncheons" (Joyce 1903, 287). The twentieth-century Bards Robert Graves and Colin Murray associated this fidh with the European Silver Fir (*Abies alba*), the tallest species of Fir tree, but there are objections to this as well: "Fir" in this context may well refer to what is, in botanical terms, Pine. There seems to be a link in Welsh tradition, for in the medieval poem "Cad Goddeu" (The Battle of the Trees) we are told of the "Pine-trees in the porch" where "the elm with his retinue, did not go aside a foot" (Skene 1868, 279). However, this species of Fir is not indigenous to the British Isles. The Irish word for a Fir tree is *giúis*. The corresponding color for *Ailm* is usually given as blue.

In the contemporary view, *Ailm* represents the towering strength that we need to rise above adversity. Like the tallest tree, we can have the viewpoint of a higher level, bringing us a better perception of future trends. If we take the Elm parallel, then it is a fidh of regeneration. The Elm can regrow from new shoots that arise from the roots. When an Elm is cut down, and seemingly dead, new stems grow from the still-living roots. This has happened in the case of trees suffering from Dutch Elm Disease.

On

On or *Onn* is the second Ogham vowel, with the phonetic value of "O," corresponding with the Gorse, Broom, or Furze (*Ulex europaeus*). This is the seventh Royal or Chieftain Tree of *An Ogham Craobh*. The modern Irish word for the Gorse is *aiteann* (Brehon Law, *aidteand*) cognate with the Welsh *eithin*. The Old Irish gloss on *Onn* is *ferus*, "Furze." The Gorse grows only in open country, not in woodland. It flowers in almost every month of the year, so it is a symbol of unending fertility. The color of *On* is that of the Gorse flowers, described variously as "golden-yellow," "saffron," "dun," or "sand." Gorse is the "plant badge" of the Scottish Logan clan.

According to contemporary interpretations, *On* signifies the carrying-on of our activities in spite of adverse surrounding conditions. This is a way of life that involves "standing out" against the background in the same way that the Gorse shows up in the landscape. Symbolically, *On* denotes the collecting together and retention of our inner strength, regardless of the outer conditions. Because the seeds of Gorse are dispersed by ants, this fidh expresses the necessity for gathering small and separate things together.

Ur

Ur or *Ura* is the third vowel, corresponding with the Heather (*Erica* sp.), in the *Book of Ballymote*, Ur. *Ur* is another problematical fidh, as Brehon Law calls this plant *freach* (modern Irish *fraoch*; Welsh *grug*). O'Flaherty's *Ogygia* calls it *Fræch*. A *Book of Ballymote* gloss also gives the correspondence *uinsenn*, "ash." *Ur* has the literal meaning of "fresh," "new," or "moist," with the associated meaning of the morning dew. Heather is considered to be an extremely lucky plant. To this day it is sold in the streets by itinerant sellers as a luck-bringer. Its traditional corresponding color is purple, the color of its flowers.

Contemporary interpretation sees *Ur* bringing good fortune and freshness to any venture to which it is applied. *Ur* serves as a portal to inner worlds. In his Druidic teachings in the Golden Section Order, Colin Murray linked this Ogham fidh with Mistletoe (*Viscum album*), as well as the Heather. He saw the Mistletoe as a complementary aspect of the fidh, signifying the power of regeneration and healing.

Edadh

Edadh or *Eadha* is the fourth vowel, phonetically "E," according to O'Flaherty's *Ogygia* "vulgarly Cranncriothach" which has been interpreted as the Aspen or White Poplar tree (*Populus tremula*). In Scottish Gaelic, the corresponding letter "e" of the alphabet is called *eadha*, whose tree is also the Aspen. The modern Irish name for the Aspen is *crithean*, and in Welsh, it is *aethnen*. The Aspen is a very hardy tree. It thrives in a diverse range of habitats, from low-lying wetlands to exposed mountain ledges. In former times, its trembling white leaves made people plant it as a very visible way- or boundary-marker.

.The esoteric view of *Edadh* is that it expresses the quality of hardihood and fierce resistance to a variety of seemingly inhospitable conditions. Thus, it is seen as a preventer of death. It facilitates our curative powers, providing direct access to the real essence that underlies the sometimes-misleading outer form. *Edadh* is the spirit than animates the flesh. At its most powerful, it signifies our willpower overriding our fate. It contains the possibility that the power of the mind can overcome the inertia of matter, warding off death.

Ida

The fidh variously called *Ida, Idha, Idad, Idho, Ioda, Ioho, Ioga*, or *Iubhar* is the Yew tree (*Taxus baccata*), with the phonetic value "I." In the Brehon Laws, it is called *ibor*. In modern Irish, it is *eo*; in Welsh, *yw*. In the Scottish Gaelic alphabet (the *aibítir*), it is *Iogh*.

The Ogham fidh is connected directly with the rune called *eihwaz* in the 24-rune Elder Futhark, which has the form of a double-ended stave of death and life. In medieval Europe, longbows, staves of death, were made of Yew. An old Irish kenning for the Yew is the "coffin of the vine," for it was from the wood of the Yew that wine barrels were made. In Scotland, the Frasers of Lovat have the Yew as their "plant badge."

The Yew is by far the longest-lived tree in Europe, evergreen throughout the year. Because of its continuity and longevity, it is seen as a tree of everlasting life, sacred to various divinities and saints of death and regeneration. In Britain, Yews are commonly trees of churchyards, the burial place of the dead. *Ida's* associated color is dark greenish-brown, the color of the tree's leaves. The under-bark and the resinous sap is blood-red, giving the phenomenon of the "bleeding Yew," where a wounded tree oozes sap, as if bleeding. Such trees are held in great veneration.

Traditional European Yew-magic deals with the mysteries of life and death: *Ida* represents the magical staff or sliver of Yew, cut at the appropriate hour, which guards against all evil. Shakespeare's *Macbeth* (VI, I) tells of the "slips of Yew, sliver'd in the Moon's eclipse," which is part of this tradition. As a time marker, it signifies the last day of the year, expressing the unity of opposites that occurs when the end of the old and the beginning of the new are present simultaneously.

The Fifth Aicme

Ida is the final vowel of the "conventional rubrics" of Ogham. The *for-feadha* ("overtrees") of the fifth aicme are diphthongs, and in modern usage, they are ascribed various meanings. Their correspondences are less well established than those of the first twenty characters, and they have a different form, being composed of complex strokes rather than the simple flesc.

Eabhadh

The first *forfidh* of the fifth aicme is the diphthong "EA," *Eabhadh*. This is interpreted as the Aspen tree (White Poplar, *Populus tremula*). This is O'Flaherty's ascription from *Ogygia*, giving it the same meaning as *Edadh* (*Eadhadh*), the fourth fidh of the fourth aicme. In Brehon Law, this tree is *crithach*. A contemporary view of this fidh gives it a quite different interpretation as *Koad*, with the phonetic value of "K." Colin Murray wrote that *Koad* signifies the unity of all eight festivals of the traditional year. He classified it as a "Grove" or "Group" rather than a tree. In this interpretation, it serves as a place for all hitherto separate things to be collected together. At such a point, all things become clear. The associated colors of *Koad* are all the "forty shades of green."

Oir

Oir has the phonetic value of "Oi," and corresponds to the Spine or Spindle tree (*Euonymus europaeus*), the eighth Royal Tree of the *Book of Ballymote*. In traditional craft, this tree provided the spindles used in spinning thread. The Spindle grows best in the milder parts of the British Isles, but, during the nineteenth century, Spindle trees were felled wholesale because the Black Bean Aphid was found to overwinter on them.

Contemporary interpretations of *Oir* view it as a fidh of destiny, coming from the tree of the spindle of the Weaving Sisters who spin, weave, and cut the thread of life. It is also seen as a fidh of childbirth, easing the passage of the baby from the womb into the world. Its associated color is white. In his Golden Section Order teachings on the Tree Alphabet, Colin Murray viewed this fidh as *Tharan*, with the phonetic value of "Th," representing a sudden flash of illumination. Murray's interpretation thus links it with the two thorn feadha, *hUath* and *Straif*.

Uilleann

The forfidh called *Uilleann* or *Uilleand* has the phonetic value of "Ui." According to the *Book of Ballymote*, this Ogham is associated with the Honeysuckle (*Lonicera* spp.) also referred to as Woodbine. Medicinally, Honeysuckle is used for treating respiratory ailments, as Nicholas Culpeper tells us in his *Complete Herbal* originally published in 1653 (1832, 308): "Honey Suckles are cleansing, consuming and digesting, and therefore no way fit for inflammations . . . it is an herb of Mercury, and appropriated to the lungs." Honeysuckle is a favorite food of goats, and its berries were formerly used to feed poultry.

In his *Ogygia*, Roderic O'Flaherty calls this fidh *Pethpoc* and tells us he has "no explanation" of its meaning. In Colin Murray's Golden Section Order teaching, it is named *Peith* and corresponds with the Guelder Rose or Snowball tree (*Viburnum opulus*), a close relative of the Wayfaring tree. It is not indigenous to Ireland. Here, *Peith* signifies an inner secret, a special dance or step that leads through the labyrinth of inner knowledge. This concept links it with the mystic *Geranos* or

"Crane Dance," performed upon labyrinths, and the crane-skin "medicine bag" that ancient Celtic magicians are said to have used to carry their magical talismans and amulets.

Ifin

According to the *Book of Ballymote*, the corresponding tree of this fidh is *Ifin*, with the phonetic value of "Io." As a tree, *Ifin* is interpreted as the Gooseberry (*Ribes grossularia*), a cultivated species that may not be indigenous to the British Isles. It appears as the Gooseberry tree *iphin* in O'Flaherty's *Ogygia*. The Welsh word for this fruit bush is *eirinen fair*, and in modern Irish, it is *spíonán*. But an "obsolete" Irish interpretation of *Ifin* is a "vineyard" (modern Irish *fíongort*). This links *Ifin* with the next fidh. Apart from being a fruit that is eaten, the Gooseberry has a medicinal function. In former times, the juice was said to cure all inflammations. The sixteenth-century herbalist John Gerard considered it a fine remedy for "hot burning ague" (1969, 138).

Again, the Golden Section Order correspondence is quite different from the *Book of Ballymote*'s Ogham Craobh. Here, Murray appears to take the *Ogham Congaine* (Consonantal Ogham) reading "PP" in Ogham "Io" (see chap. 3). This is connected with the Beech tree (*Fagus sylvatica*), and rendered as *Phagos*, with the phonetic equivalent of "Ph" or "F." The name of this tree in modern Irish is *feá*, and the Welsh *ffawydden*. Murray refers it to the solidity of ancient wisdom, the cultural or physical foundation that must be in place before any construction can be started.

Amhancholl

The final Ogham fidh is a contentious character, being ascribed four different names: *Amhancholl*, *Peine*, *Xi*, and *Mór*. It has the phonetic equivalent of "Æ." In the *Book of Ballymote*, where it is written as *Emancoll*, it is translated by Calder (1917) as "witch hazel." However, this cannot be a correct translation from a text written in 1391, because the Witch Hazel (*Hamamelis virginiana*) is a North American species that was introduced to the British Isles around the seventeenth century. What *Amancholl* means is thus open to question. As "Æ," this fidh takes the form of the grid of eight *Ifins*, which relates it to the previous fidh.

The *Book of Ballymote* infers that this is also Pine Ogham: "The figure resembles the hurdle of wrought twigs, or like a bier" (Atkinson 1874, 209). According to one version of the story "The Exile of the Sons of Uisliu," the Pines that grew over the graves of Noisiu and Derdriu, buried on opposite banks of a loch, grew toward one another and finally their branches were entwined over the loch, making a natural hurdle. In the medieval Welsh poem "Cad Goddeu" (The Battle of the Trees) we are told of the "Pine-trees in the porch, / The chair of disputation, / By me greatly exalted, / In the presence of kings" (Skene 1868, 279). In this form, *Amhancholl*'s correspondence is taken as the evergreen Scots Pine (*Pinus sylvestris*), called in modern Irish *péine* and in Welsh *pinwydden*.

Symbolically, the Pine is the tree of illumination in the darkness, recalling the traditional technique of illumination using a chip of resinous pinewood, lit at one end. Contemporary esoteric interpretation sees this fidh as the bringer of illumination, both on an intellectual and on a spiritual level. The Pine is the "plant badge" of a number of Scottish clans, including Ferguson, Fletcher, Grant, MacAlpine, MacAulay, MacGregor, and MacQuarne of Ulva.

This Ogham character has been subject to more speculative interpretation than most of them. As the twenty-fifth, it goes beyond the conventional twenty-four-fold division of things customary in the Northern Tradition (such as the Elder Futhark rune row). Therefore, it is considered to stand outside the conventions of the other twenty-four Ogham feadha, and even the other four forfeadha. So, in addition to the correspondences with Witch Hazel and Pine, this fidh has been given two further ascriptions—*Xi*, "spirit," and *Mór*, the "sea." As *Xi*, this fidh is seen as "blue-green" (or "sea-green") in color. Murray's system considered this fidh to symbolize the hidden rhythms of the ebbing and flowing tides. According to his interpretation, *Xi* is at its most powerful when the moon is full and the tide is high.

3

Ogham Cryptography, Gall Ogham, and the Gaelic Alphabet

ALTERNATIVE FORMS

The *Book of Ballymote* also presents a number of cryptic forms of Ogham. They include *Ogham Coll*, where the feadha for vowels are not composed of a series of strokes at all, but curved lines resembling the Roman letter "C." A manuscript in Trinity College describes them thus (only the vowels are given):

C—One C in *A* begins this *Ogham fine.*

CC—Two Cs, right joined in *O*, you may combine in human speech set out with taste and show.

CCC—Three Cs well formed give *U* in equal row.

CCCC—Four Cs make *E* fair seen by learning's eye.

CCCCC—Five Cs produce the ancient vowel *I*.

∪—C on its back *EA*, produces sure, nor do we err from ancient strictures, sure.

⊃C—Two Cs thus placed, the Irish *Ifin Ogain.*

∩∩—Two Cs [in] a groove, *UA* in power retain.

Ↄ—one C thus placed, *AO* in order takes.
∩—One C turned upside down *OI* bespeaks.
(Atkinson 1874, 211; slightly edited)

The "Ogham of Consonants," a version of the consonantal Ogham called *Ogham Congaine*, is another cryptic system, based on letter transference. The *Book of Ballymote* tells us that:

BH constitute A.
FT, rightly form U.
NG, bravely make I.
DL, invariably O.
SC, make E.
MM, from their backs give EA.
LL, of two Ls make IA.
BB, two Bs produce UA
PP in Ogham IO.
GG, as the directed.
(Atkinson 1874, 211)

ALTERNATIVE CORRESPONDENCES

A significant way of creating Ogham letters is to use a series of things (in the widest sense) whose names begin with different letters. The first letter of each thing is then the Ogham fidh. In the case of the trees and birds, the character of each species has a relationship with the inner meaning of its corresponding fidh. But this may not be so clear in other instances. *Lin Ogham* (Water-Pool Ogham), for instance, uses the place-names of pools of water, for example: Banba (B), Luimneach (L), Febhal (F), Sinaind (S), and Nearcnid (N). *Din Ogham* (Hill Ogham) uses terms connected with a hill to describe the feadha. *Naomh Ogham* (Saint Ogham) employs the names of Irish saints: B is Brenaid; L, Laisreann; F, Finden; S, Sinchell; and N, Neasan. H is hAdamnan; D, Donnan; T, Tigheanach; C, Cronan; and Q, Qeran (Kieran). M is represented by Manchan; G, Guirgu; Ng, Ngeman; Cr, Crannan; and R by Ruadhanachd. Finally, A is signified by An; O, Oena; U, Ultan; E, Eruan; and I, Ite.

"Battle Ogham" gives each letter to a weapon or other piece of military equipment, for example B corresponds with *Beanchor*, a horn, and numerous other objects and descriptions used in Ogham are described in the *Book of Ballymote*. The names of sciences, types of ship, herbs, meats, towns, and so forth were used in medieval Ireland, and the principle is still open to modern uses.

ALTERNATIVE NUMBERS AND ORDERS

The medieval cryptographers of Ireland devised all manner of ingenious alterations to Branch Ogham to render it unintelligible to everyone who lacked the secret key. Some of these methods may have been derived from Roman, Byzantine, or Scandinavian cryptography. Feadha can be encrypted by altering their form according to a fixed principle. The method called *Sluag Ogham* triples the number of strokes in each fidh, creating the "Ogham of the Multitudes." The "Ogham with an Additional One" adds an additional stroke to each fidh, so that they number two to six, rather than one to five strokes, for each aicme or rubric. The "Unison Ogham" writes the fidh twice each time, BB for B, and so forth. In the "Bonded Ogham" for each fidh the character next to it is written also.

The Ogham encryption called "Point toward the Pit" reverses the direction of the strokes. The A aicme reversed is in place of the B rubric, that is I for B and B for I; the M rubric reversed is in place of the H rubric; the B reversed in place of the A; and the H reversed in place of the M aicme. "End-to-end Ogham" brings together both ends of the Ogham alphabet and reorganizes its inner order. In *Ogham Bricrenn*, the "Ogham of Bricriu" (of the infamous "feast"),* the distance of a fidh from the top of the alphabet corresponds with the

---

*The Old Irish tale of "Bricriu's Feast" (*Fled Bricrenn*) tells how the protagonist invites the three greatest heroes of ancient Ulster to a feast where he sets them tasks in competition with one another. Cú Chulainn wins the contests, but the other two refuse to acknowledge him. Finally, they are all confronted by a giant who challenges them to behead him on condition that he will return the next night and do it to them. The first two do it, but flee—so when the giant returns, they have gone. Cú Chulainn finally beheads the giant and is there the next night to receive him. The giant, who is the king Cú Roí in shape-shifted form, spares Cú Chulainn and declares him supreme champion.

number of strokes written to form that single character, for example one for B and twenty for I.

The medieval Irish Oghamists reckoned the rune row of the Younger Futhark as *Gall Ogham*, the "Ogham of the Foreigner." Runic writing was introduced to Ireland by Norwegian and Danish invaders in the tenth century. An antler found in excavations in Fishamble Street in Dublin in 1980 has a Norse inscription in these runes. There is also a wooden sliver from the same district of Norse Dublin bearing the whole sixteen-rune row. In the *Book of Ballymote*, this rune row is in a different order than the standard Younger Futhark. By the time that the runes were in everyday use in Dublin a thousand years ago, the Oghams were no longer used for everyday writing.

However, even when they were no longer apparent, the Oghams flourished among scholars and poets as secret writing and signs. Medieval Oghamists encrypted names and words by changing the letter-order either within the Ogham row or in the word itself. In the "Ogham of Order," the word is arranged in the order that its feadha have in the alphabet. In *Ogham Deginach*, the "Final Ogham," the last letter of the name of a fidh is used instead of the first: S for *Luis*, and so forth. The "Ogham of Extraordinary Disturbance" puts the first letter of every aicme in place of the B aicme; the second letters for the second aicme, and so on, through the whole Ogham row of twenty-five feadha.

Some cryptic Oghams are named after the shape they take. One is the "Adder in the Heath," a strange name considering that Ireland is snakeless, indicating that this version may have related to a cryptographic system with the same name from elsewhere, as may have the system called the "Serpent [Coiled] around [Its] Head." The *Book of Ballymote* tells us:

> to write the first letter of the name in the middle of the line [or series], and to write the name from it in direct order to the end of the line, and in reversed order to the beginning of the line; so that it is the same thing that is written at the beginning and at the end of the line, that is, the end of the name is what is on either [extremity]

Variant forms of Irish Ogham as recorded in the *Book of Ballymote*.

of it. . . . With equal correctness it is to be read down and up, and it
is from the middle the name is read, for the first letter of the name
is there. (Atkinson 1874, 216)

In Ogham *Adlen Fid*, the "Struggle of the Chase" links two names.
The first half of the first name is written, then the first half of the second. They are followed by the end of the first name, and then the end
of the second.

SPATIAL DISPOSITION

Among the 150 ancient Irish Oghams are the "Wall-Fern Ogham";
"The Piercing Ogham"; "Fionn's Toothlike Ogham"; *Fege Finn* ("Fionn's
Window"); "Fionn's Wheel"; and "Fionn's Shield," which is a version of
Ogham Airenach, "Shield Ogham"). The latter four forms of Ogham
are named after the legendary Irish hero Fionn mac Cumhaill, whose
name is often anglicized to Finn McCool. Son-in-law of Cumhall mac
Trénmhoir, Fionn was the commander of the warband known as the
fiann (pl. *fianna*). According to the *Annals of Tighernach*, he was killed
in the year 284 CE. Fionn's Oghams are based on their position on concentric circles or squares within a circular or square framework. This
also allows them to be interpreted in relation to corresponding aspects
of traditional cosmology, such as the directions, times of day, or spiritual states of being.

The Ogham of "Fionn's Window" and "Fionn's Shield" is related to
the technique called *lúaithrinde* in Old Irish. This is a magical binding-
knot or optical illusion painted on a shield. One appeared on the shield
of the hero Cú Chulainn, who demanded that his shield-maker should
create an engraving unlike all others. Such patterns often created optical
illusions that had the function of distracting the opponent in combat.

The use of complementary colors in interlace patterns, such as those
in the eighth-century illuminated manuscript known as the Lindisfarne
Gospels, where red and blue are used together, was known to produce

a dazzling effect. The tesselated patterns found in Celtic and Hiberno-Saxon artwork, if painted in strongly contrasting colors, also have this effect. The Ogham colors in themselves would also spell out a message to those who could read it.

PICTORIAL AND LITERARY OGHAMS

Because each aicme of the Ogham Craobh denotes the feadha by strokes numbering between one and five, it is possible to denote the feadha by groups of other things. This gives the possibility of spelling words by sequences of pictures, or by description. There are many recorded Oghams of this kind, denoting only the first four rubrics of Ogham Craobh. As an illustration of the principle, there is the "Fawn Ogham." For the aicme of B, a stag (*dam*) is depicted: one for the first fidh, two for the second, and so on, until N is represented by five stags. The second aicme, beginning with H, is represented by one to five does (*elit*). The third aicme, beginning M, has a fawn (*iarnu*), while the fourth aicme, beginning with A, has a "sucking calf" (*laeg*). (Atkinson 1874, 217)

The "Arms Ogham" operates on exactly the same principle. A dart (*gai*) stands for the rubric beginning B; a shield (*sciath*) for H; a broadsword (*claidim*) for M; and a "good or red pointed sword" (*colg*) for the fourth aicme, beginning with A. "Human Ogham" (*Daen Ogham*) is the same. One to five men or champions stand for the first five feadha; women or clergymen for the next five, H to Q; youths for the M to R rubric; and sons or slaves for the vowels. For the four rubrics of "Dog Ogham" (*Con Ogham*) there are one to five of each of the following: collared hounds, grayhounds, pups, and lapdogs. "Ox Ogham" (*Damh Ogham*) uses bulls, oxen, a yearling, and a herd-bull, while Cow Ogham (*Bo Ogham*) has "milch cows," "strippers," "fatlings," and cows with calves. (Atkinson 1874, 212–13, 219)

The possibilities of interconnection and symbolic allusion are limitless. In former times, by such means, initiates could communicate with one another simply by mentioning the animals, birds, weapons, and so forth that corresponded with the letters. Unsuspecting listeners had no idea what they meant. The scope in symbolic prose and poetry of this sort of esoteric correspondence is immense. Any piece of literature can contain hidden messages based upon the names of things and places.

Secret visual communication was also possible when Ogham was used as a form of semaphore or sign language. These systems employed the fingers to represent the characters. It may be surmised that Ogham itself originated with these hand-signs. "Foot Ogham" (*Coir Ogham*) transmits messages by laying fingers around the foot or shinbone. They are laid, one to five, across the shinbone from the right for the aicme of B; on the left side for H to Q; diagonally for M to R; and straight across for the vowels. *Bar Ogham* is a hand-sign language that used the fingers of one hand laid across the other one to make standard or cryptic Ogham characters. In *Sron Ogham*, the fingers are laid across the central stem of the nose in the same way as for *Coir Ogham*.

COLOR OGHAM

Another visual form of Ogham is *Dathogam* ("Color Ogham"), which ascribes a color to each fidh. In Color Ogham, B is expressed by *ban*, "white"; Luis, *liath*, "gray"; F, *flann*, "crimson"; S by *sodath*, "bright," and N by *necht*, "clear." The color of Huath is also called *huath*, "terrible"; D is *dubh*, "black"; T, *temen*, "gray-green" or "dark gray"; Coll, *cron*, "brown"; and Q, *quiar*, "mousey." The next aicme begins with M, the "multicolored" *mbracht*; followed by Gort, *gorm*, "blue," and Ng, *nglas*, "yellow-green." *Straif* is represented by *sorcha*, "bright-colored," and *Ruis* by *ruadh*, "bright red." The fourth aicme is A, *alad*, "black and white"; O, *odhar*, "brownish black"; U, *usgdha*, "purple"; E, *ere*, "fox-red"; and finally, I, *irfind*, "brilliant white."

For contemporary users, *Dathogam* is difficult to use because the ancient Irish terminology of colors operates according to quite different principles of perception than are used today. Nevertheless, Color Ogham provides richly symbolic possibilities to encode written

The island of Ireland can be envisaged as "Fionn's Shield," the four
provinces corresponding with the four groups of Oghams.

meanings into artwork, abstract patterns, ornament, heraldry, fabrics, clothing, and rites and ceremonies.

Typically, the standard form of Color Ogham was not the only one. "Swine Ogham" is based on the colors of swine, as the *Book of Ballymote* tells us: "white—any shade of fairness"; "gray—any shade of gray"; "black, brown, ultra-gray, and the rest." There is also a "vessel curved underneath, a dismal habitation, worthless people [?] speckled, of a light-green colour, red [of the colour of whiteness, and the rest]; light doe colour, red doe colour, half-white or greyish-white, black, variegated" (Atkinson 1848, 221).

OBSCURE OGHAM FORMULAE

Historically, the magical use of Ogham seems to have employed certain formulae whose nature is obscure. An inscription of a magical nature is known from a stone at Glenfahan, where the letters "LMCBDV" are cut. Another cryptic inscription, "MTBCML," appears on an amber bead from Ennis, formerly used as a cure for sore eyes and to ensure safe births. It was last used by a certain Mr. Finerty, from whom it was acquired by J. H. Greaves, a jeweler from Cork. He sold it to Lord Londesborough, who gave it to the British Museum.

THE GAEILGE/GAELIC AIBÍTIR

Unlike the Oghams and Coelbrens, the Irish and Scottish aibítir (alphabet)* is actually a true *alphabet*, derived directly from Greco-Roman sources. It is related to Ogham in that the names of the *litreacha* (letters or characters, sg. *litir*) correspond similarly with trees. The Gaelic alphabet has seventeen full characters, and although there appears to be an eighteenth litir, equivalent to the Roman letter "H," it is actually ranked as an accent and not a character in its own right.

---

*Other historical variants of the word include *aibghitir* and *aiblitir*.

The Gaelic aibítir; *Y prif un awgrym ar bymtheg,* Iolo's "sixteen primary symbols"; the Awen; and other Northern Tradition alphabets, the Abcedilros, and the runic Futhark.

The Gaelic aibítir has its letters in the same order as the Roman alphabet. It is quite different from the order of the Oghams or the runes. But, as in the case of Ogham, most of the characters of the Gaelic aibítir have esoteric correspondences with specific trees. According to Shaw's *Galic and English Dictionary* (1780), which gives the letters after the tree names, the first is "*Ailm*, an Elm, the same as the letter A." Other alphabetic letters mentioned by Shaw are "*Fern*, the elder-tree, the letter F;" "*Luis*, the quicken-tree, the letter L"; "*Muin*, the thorn-tree, the letter M"; "*Nion, Nuin*, an ash-tree, name of the letter N"; "*Onn*, furze, gorse, hence the letter O"; "*Ruis*, an elder-tree, the name of the letter R"; "*Sail*, a willow-tree, a name of the letter S"; "*Tinne*, the letter T according to O'Flaherty"; "*Ur*, heath, hence the letter U takes its name"; and "*Uilleann*, honeysuckle, the name of the diphthong UI." He does not give the tree correspondences for all the characters of the *aibghitir* (as he calls it), but clearly the names of the letters are derived from their Ogham tree equivalents. Shaw's mention of O'Flaherty shows that he was familiar with the original Latin edition of *Ogygia* from 1685, as the English translation did not appear until 1793).

Perhaps because it is shorter and more limited than Ogham, the Gaelic aibítir is more coherent, possessing no awkward correspondences or herbal ascriptions that disrupt consistency. The Gaelic aibítir remains a very useful system when employed as a means of divination or for other esoteric purposes.

4

Deities of the Sacred Forest

In Pagan times, the Celtic veneration of trees was expressed sometimes in the form of gods and goddesses. Some were general deities of sacred woods or groves, while others were the gods of individual types of trees. The god Callirius Silvanus, for example, worshipped in Roman times at Colchester, appears to be a Hazel-god, (from *Coll*). The god Vernostonus, from Ebchester, has a name that is thought to mean "Alder tree" (*Fearn*), while a god called Deus Fagus (God of the Beech) was venerated in the French Pyrenees. The Gaulish god Alisanos may have been a god of the Rowan tree (*Luis*), though this interpretation is less certain; a connection has also been suggested to a Proto-Celtic word for Alder. The god Esus, otherwise called Esunertus or Esugenus, appears on the memorial pillar of the *Nautae Parisiaci*, the "Sailors of the Parisii," in Lutetia (present-day Paris), which was dedicated to Jupiter in the year 13 BCE. Here, he is depicted with an axe in his hand, pruning or cutting a tree. The Bern scholia (marginal notes) to Lucan tell that human sacrifices were made to Esus: Men were hanged on trees and stabbed at the same time so that omens could be read from the way that they bled.

Before the Romans influenced them to build temples, the Pagan Celts worshipped in holy groves of trees. Called *nemeta* (sg. *nemeton*), they were "clearings open to the sky," special places in woodland, entered only by priests and priestesses. In his *Pharsalia*, Lucan tells of the Gaulish Druids who lived in deep groves and remote uninhabited

The Water of Life, guarded by Sirona, Celtic goddess of holy wells that
contain the healing power of Apollo Grannus, the Sun,
and are often situated by a tree.

woods. His scholiast added that "They worship the gods in the woods without using temples" (Pennick and Jones 1995, 81). Much later, Christian prohibitions of the time of Charlemagne (ca. 800 CE) condemned the Pagan ceremonies in the woodlands, called *nimidas* (a term clearly related to the Celtic *nemeta*), and the *yrias*, "Pagan trackways," that linked the sacred places of the forest.* The Irish medieval tales collected and translated as the *Silva Gadelica* also tell how many sacred places of the Gaels were once groves of Hazel trees.

Many former Celtic *nemeton* sites are known today. An Old Irish name for a sacred wood is *fidnemed*, and in France, the name of the city of Nanterre recalls the Celtic place-name *Nemetodorum* ("Enduring Sacred Grove"). In England, there are the former place-names of *Vernemeton*, the "especially sacred grove," and in southern Scotland, *Medionemeton*, "Central Grove." Villages in Devon called Nympton (King's Nympton, Queen's Nympton, Bishop's Nymptom) also recall Celtic groves. Like the later temples, groves were set up or dedicated to specific deities. The Roman historian Dio Cassius (ca. 165–ca. 235 CE) reports that the Britons worshipped in groves where they sacrificed to Andraste, goddess of victory (she may be a version of Adrasteia, equivalent to the Greek Nemesis). A Gallo-Roman altar from Vaison in the Vaucluse area of south of France commemorates the establishment of a *nemeton* in honor of the goddess Belesama, who was also worshipped in Britain as the goddess of the River Mersey.

A female deity named Nemetona (Goddess of the Holy Grove) was worshiped at the great healing water shrine of Aquae Sulis (Bath) as well as Altripp, Mainz, and Trier in Germany. She was the goddess of the grove-named Nemetes tribe in the Rhine valley. In Romanized lands, Nemetona was the consort of Mars Rigonemetis, whose name means "King of the Holy Grove." Rigonemetis was also worshipped at a shrine at Nettleham near Lincoln, while the goddess Arnemetia was another deity of holy groves, worshipped at the healing springs of Buxton in the

---

*The term *nimidas* is clearly related to the Celtic *nemeta*. The source of *yrias* is unclear; it may represent a Celtic term, a Germanic one, or something else entirely.

modern Derbyshire. Another name for a holy forest is the Latin *lucus*, as in the holy forest of the tree- and spring-deity Burmanus, the *Lucus Burmani* around Cervo in Liguria, Italy. From these examples, it is clear that tree deities were a significant element in ancient Celtic spirituality.

SINGLE TREES

A lone holy tree known as *bile* grew at every holy place of inauguration of Celtic nobility. The French place-name Billom comes from the Celtic Biliomagus, the "plain of the sacred tree." Offerings and the remains of rites and ceremonies were hung in the branches of *bile* trees. Sometimes, holy trees were tended and altered to give them symbolic shapes, such as Cross Trees, Dancing Trees, and the Trained Lindens of mainland Europe. There was even an ancient Celtic god called Olloudius, whose name means "Great Tree." Remains of his worship have been found at Custom Scrubs in Gloucestershire, England, and at Antibes in the south of France. Olloudius is shown as a *genius loci* ("spirit of the place"),* dressed in a short tunic with a cloak and hood.

There were five notable venerable trees in ancient Ireland, described in the medieval onomastic text known as the *Dindsenchas* ("Lore of Places"). One tree stood for each province. They were the trees of Ross, Mugna, Tortu, Datha, and Uisnech. The branching Ash tree of Uisnech was at the omphalos of the island. It grew alongside the Stone of Division, the navel of Ireland. Mugna's tree was an evergreen Oak that bore three varieties of fruit. In addition to acorns, it produced apples and nuts, perhaps from grafted branches.

In the *Book of Leinster*, a medieval Irish poem attributed to a poet named Druim Suithe (the "Ridge of Science") about the oracular tree of Leinster, the Yew tree of Ross (*Éo Rossa*), reveals the many layers of meaning that the Celtic Bards saw in such trees:

Genius loci is Latin for the "spirit of the place," honored in various ways either as a literal spirit or figuratively as a characteristic discernable quality of a place.

Tree of Ross:
a king's wheel,
a prince's right,
a wave's noise,
best of creatures,
a straight firm tree,
a firm-strong god,
door (?) of heaven,
strength of a building,
the good of a crew,
a word-pure man,
full-great bounty,
the Trinity's mighty one,
a measure's house (?),
a mother's good,
Mary's Son,
a fruitful sea
beauty's honour,
a mind's lord,
diadem of angels,
shout of the world,
Banba's renown,
might of victory,
judgment of origin,
judicial doom,
faggot (?) of sages,
noblest of trees,
glory of Leinster,
dearest of bushes,
a bear's (?) defence,
vigour of life,
spell of knowledge,
Tree of Ross!

(Cook 1906, 66)

Symbolic trees also feature in Welsh poetry. The *Black Book of Carmarthen*, written around 1250, contains a poem beginning "*Gwin y bid y vedwen in diffrin guy . . . ,*" which translates to "Blessed is the birch in the valley of Gwy" (Skene 1868, 481). Each stanza of the poem tells of a notable Birch tree that will witness certain results of a battle in Ardudwy. Three Birches are named: that in the Valley of the Gwy; the Birch tree of Pumlumon; and the Birch on top of Dinwythwy. Another poem in *The Black Book* is called "Afallenau" (The Apple Trees). Each stanza begins with the word *afallen*, and, like the Birches, refers to trees in different locations. In it is the story of how Merlin hides in an Apple tree to escape the wrath of King Rhydderch. Merlin's trees include Apples that grow "on the edge"; "beyond the Rhun"; "in Llanerch"; "in a nook in Argoedydd"; "on the river bank"; "in grounds with various kinds of tree"; and the Apple "with flowers foxglove pink that grows in secret in the forest of Celyddon" (Pennar 1989, 67–76).

As a symbol of stability and living continuity, the Celtic battle-standard was the Oak tree. The Welsh archers who fought with the English army at Agincourt in 1415 carried images of Merlin's Oak from Carmarthen, reflecting the epithet "might of victory." John O'Donovan tells us of the ancient battlestandard of O'Loughlin, described in a manuscript:

> *In O'Loughlin's camp was visible a fair satin sheet,*
> *To be at the head of each battle, to defend in*
> *   battle-field,*
> *An ancient fruit-bearing oak, defended by a chieftain*
> *   justly,*
> *And an anchor blue, with folds of a golden cable.*
> (O'DONOVAN 1842, 350)

The Oak tree is the heraldic emblem of the O'Connors to this day. It is also the "plant badge" of clans Anderson, Buchanan, Cameron,

In Bardo-Druidic cosmology, the cosmic axis links the Welsh lower
Clych (circle) or world of Annwn with this present middle world (Abred)
and the upper worlds of Gwynvyd and Ceugant.

MacEwen, Kennedy, and Stewart. *The Royal Oak* was long a symbol of monarchist loyalty in Great Britain. One of the epithets of the Tree of Ross is "judicial doom." This is a reference to the execution of criminals and prisoners by hanging on trees. In former times in the Scottish Highlands, there were trees upon which the clan chieftains hanged their enemies. This was in exercise of their powers of "pit and gallows," the legal right to drown women in a pit and to hang men on the tree. Known as "Dool Trees" or "Grief Trees," they grew on small hillocks that were known consequently as Gallows Hills.

SACRED FORESTS AND THEIR DESTROYERS

In Pagan times, certain Celtic forests were held in reverence. The greatest of them were the Breton forests of Brocéliande and Morrois and the Scottish Wood of Caledon. Sadly, they are shadows of their former glory, for centuries of deforestation have reduced them to small remnants. In Brittany, the last remains of Brocéliande are the Forêt d'Huelgoat and the Forêt de Paimpont. Also surviving are the twin mystic woods called Coat-an-Hay and Coat-an-Noz, The "Day Wood" and "Night Wood." In Scotland, the forest known as the Wood of Caledon was once continuous from Glen Coe to Braemar and from Glen Lyon to Glen Affric. According to tradition, it was destroyed by a monster called Muime, which was brought from Scandinavia to fly over the forest and burn it down.

In reality, the Wood of Caledon was extensively cut and burnt by Scottish woodsmen between the ninth and twelfth centuries. By then, the former Pagan veneration of forests had been seriously weakened by the Christian religion. Clansmen set large tracts of woodland on fire to kill members of other clans, and to exterminate the wolves and other wild beasts that lived there. In later years, further parts of the forest fell to the shipbuilders and was burnt in the forges of ironmasters. In the twentieth century, the national emergencies of the two world wars were the excuse for yet further destruction.

In the ancient smithy, *Fearn*, the tree of fire, was an essential part of sword-making because it furnished the best charcoal for forging.

Today, the only significant remnant of this splendid Caledonian forest is the Black Wood of Rannoch at Loch Tulla. As men of the trees, the Bards were not unaware of the unfolding ecological disaster with the deforestation of Brittany, Wales, Scotland, and Ireland. The Irish Bard Aodhagán Ó Rathaille (ca. 1670–1726) lamented "Woe! your woods are withering away!" (Corkery 1925, 165–66). In Wales, the Valley sides were deforested for fuel and the animals exterminated to make way for ironworks. As an anonymous sixteenth-century Welsh Bard wrote of the destruction of Glyn Cynon Wood by English iron-workers: "There was nothing ever more disastrous than the cutting of Glyn Cynon." Once the forests were felled, men began to dig out fossil fuel from coal mines to fuel the furnaces of Wales and Scotland. Where there was little or no coal, as in Ireland, there was no "industrial revolution."

From Roman times onward, military and spiritual conquerors had been particularly intent on destroying Celtic sacred groves, which they saw as centers of native loyalty. In 49 BCE, during his civil war with Pompey, Julius Caesar destroyed a *nemeton* near Massilia (Marseille) that contained trees that had been carved into the images of goddesses and gods. In the third book of his *Pharsalia* (The Civil War), the Roman poet Lucan (Marcus Annaeus Lucanus, ca. 39–65 CE) tells how, through fear of profaning the sacred grove, Caesar's soldiers refused to cut the first tree. Then Caesar took up the axe and cried: "Believe that I am guilty of sacrilege, and thenceforth none of you need fear to cut down all the trees." He cut the first tree, and then his men followed his example, and destroyed the grove (Lucan 1928, 147).

A century later, during his persecution of British Druidry, the Roman general Suetonius Paulinus desecrated and destroyed the groves on the holy isle of Anglesey. In 452 CE, the Christian Council of Arles banned the veneration of trees, springs, and stones in southern France. The Councils of Tours in 567 CE, and Nantes in 568, extended the prohibitions in the north of France and in Brittany. Christian missionaries like Saint Martin of Tours and Saint Patrick cut down Pagan holy trees in France and Ireland, respectively. Early in the eleventh century, the Christian Irish High King (*ardrí*) Brian Boru (reigned 978–1014) took a month to cut down and burn the sacred grove of the Northmen's god, Thor, near Dublin. And in 1351, Johannes, Grand Master of the Teutonic Knights, caused the cutting down of the holy Oak tree at Romowe in East Prussia.

Because Celtic Christianity was in direct continuity with Celtic Paganism, churches were built on traditional holy places, which were Pagan. Although some missionaries like Saint Martin of Tours made it a matter of principle to cut down Pagan holy trees, it is probable that in many cases they remained when the sanctuary (Scots Gaelic *comraich*) was rededicated to the new religion. Sometimes the presence of Pagan trees has been recorded in place-names. According to his biographer, Rhygyfarch, Saint David was educated at a monastery in west Wales at Yr Henllwyn, the "Old Bush," called in Latin *Vetus Rubus*. Churches are sometimes named after trees. The church after which the town of Killarney in Ireland is named is the "church of the Blackthorn," Cill Airne. Today, ancient churchyards frequently contain venerable and venerated trees, especially ancient Yews.

TREES OF MEMORY AND INSPIRATION

As holders of ancestral heritage, the Celtic Bards were the recounters of history and genealogy. They were the writers of epitaphs and eulogies, and oversaw the rites of burial of notable people, who, as in the words of the Bard Dafydd ap Gwilym (1340–1400), "did well in their lives" (Black et al. 2015, II:160). The Bards planted trees on graves and at special locations to commemorate important events. An ancient Yew in the ruins of Strata Florida Abbey in Dyfed was planted to mark the grave of Dafydd ap Gwilym. It is a living monument to the great Bard, a tree of memory. One of the reputed graves of the wizard Merlin in Brittany, near Paimpont, is marked by a Holly tree. The tradition of record is made overt in the Irish story of the Apple and Yew that grew on the

Ogham's universal nature readily lends it to the creation of artistic and meaningful patterns. Like other Celtic art, this is a proper ornamental antidote to meaningless modernist abstraction.

grave of Bailé mac Buain and Aillinn. After seven years, we are told, the Bards cut the trees and made Poets' Tablets from them.

Isolated rows of thickly planted trees in Scotland, called "Bell Trees" (cf. *bile*) are held in great regard, for they commemorate ancestors of families and clans. Sometimes, the very fortunes of families are bound up with the fate of individual trees, such as the "Oak of fate from the wood" (Atkinson 1874, 209). For example, the great tree growing at Howth Castle in Ireland was linked with the St. Lawrence family, the Earls of Howth. We find the same tradition in Great Britain. In Scotland, at Dalhousie Castle, near Edinburgh, grew the Edgewell Tree. The destiny of the Edgewell family was said to depend upon the condition of this tree. Another famed Scottish tree, the Oak of Errol, bore a Mistletoe plant whose fate was bound up with the Hays of Errol in the Carse of Gowrie. In his book *Forest Folklore*, Alexander Porteous quotes a member of the Hays, writing of the *geas* ("taboo"; Irish Gaelic *geis*) in 1822:

> the duration of the family of Hay was said to be united with its existence. . . . The two most unlucky deeds which could be done by one of the name of Hay was, to kill a white falcon, and to cut down a limb from the Oak of Errol. (Porteous 1928, 230)

In England it was said that the Fulford family, living near the Cornwall-Devon border, held their lands on condition that once a year they dined upon the platform in the branches of the great Oak at Dunsford, and held a dance there for their tenants.

Similarly, the state of Merlin's Oak in Carmarthen, Pembrokeshire, west Wales, was said to reflect the condition of the town. This was a very famous tree, for the Welsh archers who gave the strategic advantage to the King of England's army at the Battle of Agincourt in 1415 carried images of Merlin's Oak for luck. In the nineteenth century, Merlin's Oak was killed deliberately by a religious fanatic who disapproved of the crowds that congregated there day and night. For many years afterward, the Oak's lifeless bole stood in the street, in latter times propped up by concrete and iron. Sadly, no attempt was made to plant a new tree, and eventually, to make room for more traffic, the dead trunk was transported to the museum. This was ironic, considering the tradition that the spirit of the town was embodied in Merlin's living tree: "When Merlin's Oak shall tumble down, Then shall fall Carmarthen town."

In 1745 the Jacobite Bard Alasdair mac Mhaighstir Alasdair (Alexander MacDonald) planted an Oak at Dalilea House at Moidart in Scotland, in celebration of the return of Bonnie Prince Charlie in his attempt to regain the throne for the Stuarts. In the next century, whole plantations were made on estates all over Scotland to commemorate the victory of the British Army over Napoleon at the Battle of Waterloo. The shapes and spatial relationship of plantations in the landscape reproduced the disposition of the military units in the battle. They still exist on the promontory at the eastern entrance to the Kyles of Bute at Loch Striven, and as the Glenearn Woods by the Bridge of Earn in Tayside. The custom was continued in 1948, when a wood in the shape of a crown was planted at Rothesay on the Isle of Bute to celebrate the birth of the heir to the throne of the United Kingdom, Prince Charles.

Trees are living beings whose ensoulment makes them perfect media through which we can draw inspiration. The intimate relationship between Bards and trees is evident throughout history. The mad Merlin in his Apple tree, the Oghams, the Tablets of the Poets, and the "wattles and branches" of Welsh poetry are among the many manifestations. Thus, specific trees are associated with places of learning. In 1458 William Waynflete, Bishop of Winchester, founded Magdalen College at Oxford. It was located in the shadow of the Great Oak, which lived until 1788. The Caerwys Tree in north Wales is actually an authentic Bardic tree of inspiration. The present tree is a Sycamore, planted in the mid-twentieth century to replace the earlier one, which had perished. From 1568, when Queen Elizabeth I authorized the first official Eisteddfod (Bardic session) at Caerwys, competing Bards sat around the base of the tree to compose, then walked across the road to perform their new poems at the Eisteddfod hall.

FRUIT-BEARING TREES

Although they destroyed Pagan holy trees and groves, some Celtic Christians were also planters. In sixth-century-CE Brittany, the British monks Teilo and Samson "planted a great grove of fruitbearing trees, to the extent of three miles, from Dól as far as Cai" (Baring-Gould and Fisher 1913, 4:161). To this day, Saint Teilo is the patron of Apple trees. In former times in Wales, all trees growing on land dedicated to Saint Beuno were considered sacred, and were never cut or damaged in any way. In the medieval text called "The Essentials of a Physician," the physicians of Myddfai deemed it necessary that a medical practitioner should have "A garden of trees and herbs, where such herbs, shrubs and trees, as do not everywhere grow naturally, may be kept cultivated, and where foreign trees and plants, which require shelter and culture before they will thrive in Wales, may be grown" (Pughe 1865, 460).

The present veneration of apple orchards by many people is a continuation of the ancient respect for sacred groves. In Herefordshire, it was the custom that if a man wanted to take over a piece of common land, he must first plant an apple tree there. From medieval times, the *Privileges* of the Free Miners of the Forest of Dean, Cornwall, and elsewhere have permitted them to prospect for, and extract coal and minerals in areas where they were plentiful. Their Royal Charters, which have precedents in ancient Welsh law, give the Free Miners the right to dig on any land, with three exceptions. They may not dig up the Queen's Highway, consecrated churchyards, or orchards of fruit-bearing trees.

Writing in *The Folk-Lore of Herefordshire*, Ella Mary Leather comments (1912, 20):

The apple is our Herefordshire tree *par excellence*; the old labourers look upon the destruction of an orchard almost as an act of sacrilege, and they say that if an orchard be cut down to plant a hopyard, it will never pay the cost of cultivation.

The tradition continues in many parts of England and Wales of wassailing the orchards, often on Twelfth Night (January 6), when offerings of bread and cider or ale are made to apple trees. Cider may be poured over the roots, shotguns are fired three times through the branches, fireworks and party poppers are let off, drums are beaten, traditional wassail songs are sung, and the health of the trees drunk in cider and other strong beverages.

RENEWAL

Like all living things, trees have a limited life, so when a notable tree dies, it is customary to plant a new one in its place. The new tree should be grown from a cutting of the old one, or, if this is not possible, from a seedling of its fruit. In this way, the old tree is reborn in its original location, and continuity can be possible over thousands of years. But when this principle is not understood, and the old, dead, tree is preserved as a relic, then the opportunity to plant anew is lost. Eventually, the remains of the dead tree will disintegrate with time or be removed. Then the place ceases to be special. This happened at Carmarthen in west Wales, where Merlin's Oak was not replaced by a new one. However, all is not lost, for the tradition does continue in many places, such as at Caerwys. At Lillington, near Leamington Spa, one of the places reputed to be the center of England, grew a tree called the Midland Oak. When it died in 1982, a new tree was planted to replace it. Similarly, the Arbour Tree, a flag-bedecked Poplar at Aston-upon-Clun in Shropshire, was replanted in the mid-1990s. Whenever such a notable old tree perishes, it is necessary that local people keep up the tradition, and plant another for the enjoyment of future generations.

"GREEN MEN": MEN AND WOMEN OF THE TREES

The name *Green Man*, describing foliated faces in medieval churches, was first used as recently as 1939 by Lady Raglan in an article in the

Merlin, the archetypal Celtic wise-but-wild-man who lives at the
boundaries of the human, animal, and plant realms.

journal *Folklore*. It is used almost universally today to describe any face surrounded by leaves in various ways or even formed entirely of leaves. They appear as building ornament, sacred or secular, as well as in medieval manuscripts. Such images of human faces in foliage can be traced back into Celto-Roman times. They appear to represent several different mythic and legendary beings. The Gaulish god Erriapus, who is known best from the Garonne region of France, is depicted on an altar from Saint-Béat as a head emerging from foliage. "Leaf masks" also appeared in Roman art during the first century CE. A foliated face, seemingly a water-being, perhaps the god Neptune, forms the center-piece of the great silver dish dated to the mid-fourth century CE, found with other Roman remains at Mildenhall in Suffolk.

A fragment of Roman masonry from a demolished second-century Gallo-Roman temple seems to have played a significant role in the development of the architectural "green man." It was incorporated into the sixth-century-CE cathedral at Trier in the Rhineland. It bore a foliated "leaf mask" that may have influenced church builders in the "Romanesque" style elsewhere, becoming a widespread ornamental motif. Fragments of the medieval tomb of Saint Frideswide in Oxford Cathedral show her face amid foliage. These images refer to the story of how she hid in the forest when hunted by an unwelcome suitor. Other images show beings with branches or leaves emanating from nostrils or mouth, or forming the hair or beard. This type of medieval "Green Man" was the subject of an exhaustive study by Kathleen Basford pub-lished in 1978, titled *The Green Man*.

The "Wild Man" or "Woodwose" was a popular character in medi-eval pageants, *Pas d'Armes*, tournaments, and carnivals, and appears today at *Fastnacht* (Shrovetide) and in autumnal festivals in various parts of south Germany, Switzerland, and the Tyrol. The inventory of the properties for the Feast of the Nativity at Otford in Kent in 1348 includes "XII wildmen's heads" (masks). The tournament called the *Pas d'Armes de la Sauvage Dame*, held in Ghent (Flanders) in 1469, was opened by two "Wild Men" with trumpets and two others, leading richly caparisoned horses on which rode two "Wild Ladies," carrying the prizes for the victor.

In the Alpine region, Wild Men and Women are said to symbolize the spirit of free, natural life, bringing strength, health, and fertility. Guisers dressed as "Wild Men" and "Wild Women" are recorded from the *Schempartlauf* in Nuremberg in 1470, 1539, and the eighteenth century. The wild people of the Älplerchilbi festival in Switzerland are recorded as far back as 1624. In Great Britain, in the reign of King James VI and I, the men whose job it was to let off fireworks at celebrations were called "Green Men." John Kierke's play *The Seven Champions of Christendome* has the line (1638, sig. H2): "Have you any squibs in your Country? any Green-men in your shows . . . ?"

The story of *Valentine and Orson* appears first in a French romance of 1489. It tells of twin brothers, born in a wood at Orleans and separated at birth when Orson is carried off by a she-bear. The bear raises him with her cubs, and he becomes a wild man, while Valentine is raised as a nobleman. The play takes place when they meet, years later, and Orson is captured during a hunt. Later, Orson overthrows the Pagan Green Knight and marries Fezon, daughter of Duke Savary of Aquitaine.

Peter Breugel's painting *The Battle of Carnival and Lent* (1559) shows the story of *Valentine and Orson* being performed as a mummers' play in a village street. Orson is clad in vegetation as a Wild Man and carries a club. The story was still well known in the nineteenth century, when a mural of Orson and Valentine was painted in Cardiff Castle. In Central Europe, the wild man appears in the *Wildmannspiel* ("Wild Man's Game") and *Wildmanntanz* ("Wild Man's Dance") in connection with driving out winter. At Kandersteg in Switzerland, for instance, the New Year guisers called *Pelzmarti* include a man called the Chrismaa. He is dressed from head to foot in branches of the Fir tree (Bärtsch 1993, 55–56). Also bedecked with Fir branches are the masked Wild Men and Women called *Osemali* who appear during *Fasnet* at Tannheim in the Schwarzwald region of south Germany. Another kind of "Green Man" appears in the midwinter *Perchtenlauf* of Pongau in Austria, where men called *Verchmanndl*, with blackened faces and dressed from head to foot in green lichens, climb on house roofs and push snow down upon unsuspecting bystanders.

The archetypal Celtic wizard, Merlin, is also part of this complex motif of humans-in-trees. In the aforementioned Welsh poem "Afallenau" (ca. 1250), we are told how, having lost his wits from witnessing the slaughter of battle, Merlin enters the Wood of Caledon. There, he becomes a wild man who hides in an Apple tree when he is hunted by King Rhydderch. Salaün ar Foll ("Salomon the Fool"), the divine madman of Le Folgoët in Brittany, a devotee of Our Lady who died in 1358, used to sit up in a tree above a holy well, praying.

The motif of the human face in the tree was adopted in Restoration England for the inn, tavern, alehouse, and public-house sign *The Royal Oak*. This symbol arose in 1651, when, following his defeat in battle at Worcester, King Charles II fled and was hunted by parliamentary soldiers. He escaped detection by hiding amid the branches of the great Oak tree at Boscobel in Worcestershire. After the restoration, the tree was revered by royalists as "The Royal Oak," savior of the British monarch.

The actual tree died in 1704 as the result of continuous depredations by relic-hunters. A descendant of the Royal Oak grows at Boscobel today. *The Royal Oak* remains as a popular name for inns throughout England, where the king's head is portrayed amid the foliage. The festival called *Royal Oak Day* or *Oak Apple Day*, May 29th, commemorates the restoration of King Charles II to the throne in 1660. It is customary to wear Oak leaves on that day, and a festival is held at Great Wishford in Wiltshire. There it is celebrated with a procession and dancing, followed by ceremonial Oak-branch cutting.

In his monumental list (1864), the authority on English inn signs, Jacob Larwood, numbers twenty-four inns, taverns, and public houses called Green Man in London alone. Larwood suggested that the *Green Man* sign was "perhaps originally *Jack-in-the-Green*; in other instances *Archer* or *Robin Hood*." He thought that the sign *Wild Man* may have also been derived from these two:

The Green Man, whose mask appears in medieval churches
throughout western Europe, is a significant figure in
contemporary Paganism.

The Royal Oak, showing the face of King Charels II in the Boscobel Oak, is a favorite English inn and public-house sign.

For the sign of the *Green Man* there is a twofold explanation. I:—
That it represents the green, wild, or wood men of the shows and
pageants, such as described by Machyn in his Diary on Lord May-
or's Day, 1553, and in the account of the festivities when Queen
Elizabeth was at Kenilworth Castle in 1575. Besides wielding sticks
with crackers in pageants, these green men sometimes fought with
each other, attacked castles and dragons, and were altogether a
very popular character with the public. 2:—The second version of
this sign is, that it is intended for a forester, a verderer or ranger,
and in that garb the *Green Man* is now almost invariably represented. (Larwood and Hotten 1951, 221–22)

Corroborating Larwood, as early as the seventeenth century, London
trade tokens bore images of the "Green Man" as a forester. Robin Hood,
dressed in his outlaw's livery of Lincoln Green (or, occasionally Kendal
Green), also appeared as the "Green Man."

Some believe the inn sign *The Green Man* to be derived from the
heraldic arms of the Distillers' Company, which was founded as a
Livery Company of the City of London in 1709 (and ranks 87th in
precedence). The supporters of the arms are two "Indians" (Native
Americans), for which sign painters frequently substituted foresters or
"wild men." Larwood notes that *The Green Man and Still* in White
Cross Street, London, once had a sign showing a forester drinking
"drops of life" (*Aqua vitae*).

Another theory comes from Brewer, in *The Dictionary of Phrase
and Fable*, where he states that the inn sign *The Green Man and Still*
refers to the distillation of spirits from green herbs, such as Peppermint
Cordial (1900, 552). The "Green Man" in this meaning is thus the
"Greengrocer of Herbs," and the still is the apparatus in which the
liquor is distilled.

Many *Gasthäuser* (inns) in south Germany, northern Switzerland,
and Austria are also called after the Wild Man—*Zum Wilden Mann*.
Until they were driven out of business by modem medicine, Central

In many ways, the wizard Merlin, the wild orphan Orson, and
King Charles II are aspects of the Woodwose, or Wild Man, here shown
wrestling with a unicorn, symbol of purity.

European herbalists, mountebanks, and quacks traveled through the land accompanied by assistants dressed as "Wild Men." This was done both as a means of advertising and as authentication of their potions and lotions, powders and pills, some of which were made by distilling herbs. During the eighteenth century, the Bavarian authorities felt that these traveling medicine men were a menace, and so guising as the "Wild Man" was prohibited by law. Perhaps there was once a similar connection with medicinal cures and this guiser in Britain. In the nineteenth century, the *Green Man* public house in Edgware Road, London, possessed a medicinal spring in its cellars, from which "eye lotion" was provided, free of charge, to customers.

Lady Raglan's 1939 article linked her "Green Man" with the figure of English traditional performance known as Jack-in-the-Green. The custom of Jack-in-the-Green is practiced on May Day each year, when a man is dressed from head to foot in fresh green leaves and then parades with the morris dancers and other guisers in procession through the streets. Historically, as a May Day practice in England, Jack-in-the-Green cannot be traced back earlier than the eighteenth century, when the chimney sweeps, especially in London, paraded on their traditional holiday, (described by Roy Judge in his influential study, *The Jack-in-the-Green* [1979]). A painting by John Collett, titled *May Morning* (circa 1760) shows a May Day parade in London. It does not show a Jack-in-the-Green, but milkmaids carrying bright copperware and silverware on their heads. Of course, Jack's absence here is not evidence of absence on that day elsewhere in London or anywhere else. A later London May Day painting, *Upper Lisson Street* (ca. 1837–47), shows a fully leafed Jack-in-the-Green with a floral crown on the apex of his costume, accompanied by a drummer, a blackened-faced boy, a ribbon-bedecked man, and a Harlequin-like character with a mask. The relationship of Jack-in-the-Green with his "Wild Men" counterparts in English and continental pageants is still to be fully investigated.

As leaf-bedecked people walk or dance through the streets of village, town, and city, their leaves are shed, symbolically spreading their

The Straw Bear, paraded annually in January at Whittlesey in
Cambridgeshire (with part of the traditional tune behind). Guising in
vegetation on special festival days of the year is an ancient tradition
maintained in many places across Europe.

new greenery. As a springtime manifestation of fertility, this parallels the grains and straw dropped by the Straw Bears of Whittlesey in England, Walldürrn, Wilflingen, and over fifty other locations elsewhere in Germany as they drive out winter and herald the coming growing season. Jacks-in-the-Green appear today in a major May festival at Hastings in Sussex, the Rochester Sweeps' Festival in Kent, in Oxford for the May Morning celebrations, and in many other places. A contemporary song in English traditional style, "Jack-in-the-Green," written by Martin Graebe, is often performed along with the guising. At present, the "Green Man" is a potent image in contemporary Paganism, where it represents a god of vegetation.

5

Celtic Tree Lore of Birch, Thorn, and Oak

BIRCHES OF MAY AND SUMMER

Although the custom remains most vigorous today in mainland Europe, May Trees and their allies were set up in former times all over the Brythonic lands. As the primary tree, the Birch was favored. A whole tree was cut down on May Eve. Then it was transported to the nearest village or town and set up. Its presence there on May Day was deemed necessary if fertility and prosperity were to crown the coming season. For a short time, the May Tree recreates the forest within the town, bringing back to it the wild spirit of growth.

Traditions of Celtic festive trees are best recorded from Wales and along the Welsh borderlands in England. One of the earliest references we have is a fourteenth-century *cywydd* (metrical verse) from the Bard Grufydd ap Adda ap Dafydd (ca. 1352–ca. 1382), who laments the fate of a Birch that has been cut down to be the May Tree at Llanidloes. He contrasts its proper place, growing in the wood, with its new temporary location by the town's pillory.

In south Wales, the ceremony of setting up the May Tree is called *codi'r fedwen*, "raising the birch." In north Wales, it is *y gangen haf*, "the summer branch." It is traditional to bedeck *y gangen haf* with the most

100

precious possessions of the village, such as pocket watches, brooches, silver tankards, and dishes. In the eighteenth century, William Robert o'r Ydwal, the "Blind Poet of Llancarfan," described the raising of the Birch in his poem "Taplas Gwainfo" (The Taplas of Wenvoe). The pole was trimmed by a carpenter until it was round, and then it was decorated with pictures. Young women then adorned it with ribbons and wreaths. A weathercock with ribbons streaming from its tail was set on its apex, beneath which a banner was unfurled. Morris dancing, *dawns y fedwen* (the "Dance of the Birch") was performed beneath such May Trees. Before the Great War put an end to the custom, Herefordshire farmers felled a tall thin Birch on May Day. They bedecked it with ribbons and set it up against the stable door to bring good luck for that year.

In addition to setting up Birchen Maypoles, Welsh custom also erects *y fedwen haf,* "the Summer Birch." This is set up on the feast of Saint John at Midsummer (June 24th). European tradition does not restrict pole-erection to May or Midsummer. In Wales three poles, painted red, white, and green, are set up next to the road at the entrances of a village where an Eisteddfod is being held. At the Shrovetide festival of *Fastnacht* in south Germany, villages erect the *Narrenbaum* (Fools' Tree), identical with Maypoles except that they are bedecked with rags, and sometimes comic objects like chamber pots. They are cut down ceremonially on Shrove Tuesday. Other trees or poles are erected at Easter, Whitsun, and Harvest, and the Christmas Tree, first brought into Britain from Germany and popularized in 1841 by Queen Victoria's husband, Prince Albert, is universal.

Although it has largely lapsed, there is an identical custom of the Midsummer Pole in Cornwall. A description of the tradition formerly kept up until 1725 in the Capel Hendre district of Llandybie in Carmarthenshire tells of the scale of the Midsummer revels around the Birch:

> The dance was to begin on St. John's Day and to continue, if the weather were favourable, for nine days. There were one or two harpists, and the assembly, both male and female, used to dance.

They used to set a birch tree in the earth and decorate its branches
with wreaths of flowers. (Owen 1959, 110)

In medieval Wales, lovers' bowers were made beneath Birch trees,
and wreaths of Birch were given as tokens of love. "Before there was the
law of a pope or his trouble," *The Red Book of Hergest* tells us:

> *Each one made love,*
> *Without blame to his loved one.*
> *Free and easy enjoyment will be without blame,*
> *Well has May made houses of the leaves—*
> *There will be two assignations, beneath trees, in*
> *   concealment,*
> *For me, myself and my dear one.*
>
> (REES AND REES 1967, 287)

All over Europe, it is customary for the men of neighboring par-
ishes to attempt to cut down or steal their neighbors' Maypole. If they
succeed, then they have brought shame on the village whose pole is lost.
Writing in 1842, Morgan Rhys noted:

> It was considered a great disgrace for ages to the parish that lost
> its birch, whilst on the other hand, the parish that succeeded in
> stealing a decked bough, and preserving its own, was held up in
> great esteem . . . no parish that had once lost its birch could ever
> hoist another, until it had succeeded in stealing one that belonged
> to some of the neighbouring parishes. (Owen 1959, 109)

Such Maypole destruction continues in Germany today, when the local
youths are not sufficiently vigilant against those of neighboring villages
for three nights after the pole is set up.

In Wales, the custom was accompanied by considerable vio-
lence. The diary of William Thomas (1727–1795), who lived at

Michaelston-super-Ely, near St. Fagans in the Cardiff region, tells of the attempted theft of the Summer Birch in June 1768. The villagers of St. Fagans were compelled to use firearms to protect their Birch against a mob of fifty men from nearby St. Nicholas. A day or two later, the St. Nicholas men were joined by others from Llancarfan and Penmark, so the defenders called in reinforcements from Llandaff and Cardiff.

Besoms

Throughout Europe, besoms are far more than just utilitarian brooms for sweeping the floor. They are both revered and feared, having a part in many customs and traditions. In the British Isles, the original besoms are believed to have been made from the Broom plant (the Ogham *On*). The traditional English besom is made from three woods. The actual broomstick or *stale* is made of Ash, to which an array of Birch twigs are tied with osiers (Willow). Thus, in Ogham terms, the besom is made from *Nin*, *Beith*, and *Saille*, three feadha of the first aicme, and all Kiln or Peasant Trees.

In former times in East Anglia, the broom-tiers or *Broom Squires* made the brush-end of brooms from Ling (Heather), bound to the broomstick by long pliant bonds of split Bramble. In Ireland, it was customary to use a Heather besom to sweep the threshing-floor, and in Scotland, a Heather broom, called the "Broom-Cow," is used in the game of Curling, for sweeping the ice in front of the moving stones. Occasionally, the twigs that compose the besom proper are made of Hazel (*Coll*) or Rowan (*Luis*), but Birch (*Beith*) is the best.

Generally, the besom has the apotropaic function of keeping out unwanted people or harmful supernatural beings. A Romani tradition recorded in Hampshire asserted that if an "ill wisher" approached one's dwelling, then a besom laid across the threshold would prevent entry. Irish custom asserts that for protection against all mishaps, a broom should be leaned against the dairy door while the milk is being churned. According to French folk wisdom, because the besom sweeps away bad things, gradually it accumulates dirt and harmful powers, and becomes bad in itself. It then has the possibility to be used for evil purposes by malevolent individuals. Therefore, like most Maypoles, a fresh broom should be made each year.

Times of year for making new brooms vary from place to place. They vary from Twelfth Night in Westphalia and Mecklenburg, Germany; springtime in Switzerland; Easter in Old Bohemia (Czech Republic); St. George's Day (April 23rd) in Austria; and Midsummer Day (St. John's Day, June 24th) in Rome. In England it is considered inauspicious to make a new broom of Birch twigs or green Broom during the Twelve Days of Christmas or in the merry month of May. It is unlucky to sweep the house at all in May, for it will bring death: "If you sweep the house with broom in May, You'll sweep the head of the house away."

In German-speaking countries, besoms are not be left outside on Walpurgis Night (May Eve), because they might be used by witches who roam abroad on that night.

Just as the time of making new brooms is significant, so certain dates are considered important in sweeping-lore. Traditions of sweeping at New Year persist in northern England. At Laneshaw Bridge, near Colne in Lancashire, it is customary to sweep the old year out and the new year in. In former times, men, women, and children went round from house to house on New Year's Eve between ten o'clock and midnight. Disguised with masks or blackened faces, the sweepers had the right to enter any house whose door was not fastened. If they encountered a locked door, they made a "mumming" sound to encourage those inside to open up. Without a word or a song, the sweepers entered the part of the house where the family was and dusted the room and the hearth. When they finished, they rattled their money-boxes and received largesse. In Handsworth, Sheffield, a mummer personating "Little Devil Doubt," carrying a besom, sweeps out the houses.

In comes I, Little Devil Doubt,
If you don't give me money,
I'll sweep you all out.

Money I want, and money I crave.
If you don't give me money,
I'll sweep you all to your grave!

proclaims the besom-wielding Little Devil Doubt in the mummers' play *The Old Tup* (version from Ecclesfield, Sheffield, 1893).

It is said in Eyam, Derbyshire, that unless one sweeps the doorstep on the first of March, then the house will be infested with fleas for the rest of the year. In Cambridge, the first of March was called "foe-ing out day." The house was swept, and a protective pattern chalked upon the front doorstep.

Sweeping magically with the besom is similar to sweeping dirt, except that luck is being swept rather than physical dust and detritus. *Fastnacht Narrenzünfte* (Fools' Guilds) in many places in south Germany include "witches" with besoms who sweep away bad things, evil, and winter. Traditional witchcraft in western England uses a besom or broom bundle made of Broom to sweep the circumference of "magic circles" in which rituals are conducted. The besom has long been the emblem of the witch. In Ireland in 1323, Alice Kyteler of Kilkenny was brought before a court, accused of being a witch. An allegation made against was that she:

> swept the streets of Kilkenny between complin and twilight, raking all the dung towards the door of her son, William Outlaw, murmuring and muttering all the while secretly between her teeth, these words—"To the house of William, my son, Hie all the wealth of Kilkenny town." (Oufle 1830, 587)

By so doing, it was thought, she could accumulate others' riches magically in her son's house. Custom in the British Isles demands that dust should always be swept inward across the threshold. If the sweeper should sweep the dust outward, then she will sweep away the luck of the house. When the out-sweeper is a bride sweeping the house for the very first time, then disaster will follow.

The four faces of the ninth-century Celtic cross at Nevern in
Pembrokeshire, with interlace and key-patterns that reflect the "wattles
and the branches" of British Bardic tradition.

In England and Wales, a besom is used to solemnize the customary common-law wedding. A Birch-twig besom must be propped up across an open doorway, either the bride's home, or another place in which the couple intend to live together. The man leaps over the broom into the house, followed by his bride. When they jump, they must touch neither the doorpost nor the broom. If this should happen, then the ceremony is invalid. "Jumping the broomstick" must be performed in the presence of witnesses who ensure that the proper form is observed, and no touching takes place. Traditionally, formal separation can take place within twelve months of "jumping the broomstick" by reversing the ceremony, and jumping out of the house over the besom, again in the presence of witnesses. The British Romani tradition also employs besoms in marriage ceremonies. Romani brides and grooms use a besom made from flowering Broom, which they lay on the ground. The couple, holding hands, jump backward over it. An alternative rite sees the father of the bride holding a besom, which the couple, man first, leap over.

According to English traditional usage, a woman who wants to tell others that she is away from home places her broom stick against the door, with its twigs upwards, or, more rarely, protruding from the chimney. But this sign is said to give the husband or partner the freedom to associate with other women while the broom is up. Thus the expression "to hang out the besom" means for a man to have a sexual relationship with another woman while his wife is absent. Similarly, in France, the expression "*rotir le balai*" (to "burn the besom") means to live a sexually promiscuous life. The English traditional songs "Green Brooms" and "The Besom-Maker" suggest that the trade of broom-cutting has erotic undertones.

The history of sexual arousal through birching is poorly documented. The earliest publications on the subject in English appear to be *The Birchen Bouquet* (1780) and *Venus, Strict Mistress of Birchen Sports* (1788). In his *English Eroticism* (1984), Piero Lorenzoni estimates that around one hundred books about sexual birching were published in England in the nineteenth century. These included *Colonel Spanker's Experimental Discourse* (1836), which tells of the exploits of the "Society of Aristocratic Flagellants" in London's Mayfair, and Margaret Anson's book on an exclusively female secret society called *The Merry Order of St. Bridget* (1857), whose initiations and ceremonies involved birching.

Thus, the Birch is a symbol of sexuality, fertility, and growth. It is said that children must never be chastised with besoms or they will not grow. It was once believed that if an unmarried woman stepped across a besom on the ground, she would become an unmarried mother. At times of "misrule"* it was not uncommon in the past for naughty boys to place brooms at strategic places in the house where girls would cross them unknowingly. In Yorkshire to this day, calling a woman a "besom" is an insult, meaning that she has borne a child out of wedlock, the result of a "greenwood marriage," and in southern Scotland, a prostitute is called a "besom."†

FAIRY THORNS, GENTLE TREES, AND OUR LADY'S TREE

Celtic lore tells of trees and bushes whose unusual outward form expresses an inner spiritual quality. Irish vernacular tradition recognizes that any lone Thorn tree growing in the middle of a stony field, or on a hillside, is the property of the fairies. Such trees are deemed especially venerable when they are growing by a large boulder or over a holy well. Also, Thorn trees that grow upon a hedge- or field-bank denote a fairy place. When three or more Thorn trees grow together naturally to form an L- or V-shape, then they have done so under otherworldly influence. It is believed that otherworldly beings are present in certain trees.

---

*At Hallowe'en and several other days in specific localities, "mischief nights" were formerly times when transgressive acts were expected and tolerated.

†According to Iolo Morganwg's poetic ideas, the besom is symbolic of the twigs and branches of the Bardic Coelbren alphabet (see chap. 6), where it is called *Y Ddasgubell Rodd*. This is the "Gift Besom" that symbolizes the sweeping away of everything that conceals the truth. A Bardic text of uncertain date, published in 1866, gives a teaching concerning the Ddasgubell Rodd as a key to the "Primitive Coelbren." Here, as in its physical aspect, the besom is a symbol of transition, the creator of change.

According to Cornish lore, people who buried treasure always planted a Hawthorn over it. This prevented the *piskies* (pixies) from taking it away. In Ireland, the sprites called *Lunantishees* guard the Blackthorn (*Straif*) bushes from unwarranted interference.

The holy Thorn trees known as "Gentle Bushes" play an important part in vernacular religion. They are protectors of the locality, bringing the best possible fortune. Thorns play an important role in local lore. The Irish Bard Raftery sang the praises of the Killeaden Fairy Thorn of Lis Ard, and Saint Senán lay down to die under a Thorn tree at Kileochaille near Rossbay, County Clare. As he was dying, he said "Let me lie here till dawn," and so his body was allowed to rest beneath the Thorn until the sun rose again (Baring-Gould and Fisher 1913, 4:192).

Fairy Thorns should never be cut or damaged, even the fallen leaves and branches lying beneath them should not be taken away. Sometimes, a branch broken off accidentally will be tied back into its original position, rather than being removed. "Don't tamper with the lone bus," we are warned, for it is considered extremely unlucky to destroy a sacred tree. In former times, deep respect for these trees was a universal geis. If, for some reason, deliberate or accidental, the geis was broken, then appalling misfortune would befall the geis-breaker. In addition to this, people, animals, plants, and property in the locality of the tree would suffer. To fell a fairy tree is to risk releasing harmful forces that it holds in check. The resulting imbalance can take the form of poor crops, sickness in humans and animals, and general misfortune. Only by planting a new tree of the same species at that place, using the proper rites and ceremonies, may the imbalance be rectified.

The lone Thorn tree that grows on Wearyall Hill at Glastonbury, visible for miles around, is a typical "fairy tree." The current Thorn is the descendent of a miraculous tree that legendarily had been planted by the first Christian in Britain, Joseph of Arimathea. The "original" Thorn had two stems. In the early seventeenth century, one was cut down by a religious fanatic, who was punished immediately for his sacrilege. In *Dodona's Grove* (1644), James Howell wrote:

> He was well serv'd for his blind Zeale, who going to cut doune
> an ancient white Hauthorne-tree, which, because she budded be-
> fore others, might be an occasion of Superstition, had some of the
> prickles flew into his eye, and made him Monocular.

The rest of the Thorn was cut down by Cromwell's followers. But by then, devout people had taken the precaution of growing new bushes from cuttings, and a descendant still grows in the churchyard of St. John's in Glastonbury High Street. Like its forebears, it blossoms around midwinter, and cuttings are sent to the reigning monarch. Others grow in various parts of England, and blossom at the same time.

Dermot MacManus recounts in his book *The Middle Kingdom* (1958) the story of the Thorn tree that was cut down to clear the ground for a new hospital at Kiltimagh. Although he was warned not to do it, the workman felled the Thorn, only to suffer a stroke which led to his death. The place at which this occurred was considered to be cursed by the sacrilege, and the building erected there never served as a hospital. Many years later, in the early 1970s in Ulster, a Fairy Thorn was cut down because the "greenfield site" was required to build a new car factory. It was the place of manufacture of the ill-fated DeLorean car, which cost the taxpayer dearly when it went out of business shortly after production commenced.

That trees can be the receptacle of spirit is demonstrated by the holy well of Saint Fintan at Clonenagh in County Laois, Ireland. This, "holy well" was halfway up a tree. Of course, according to literalist perceptions, a tree cannot contain a well, for no water can flow from it. But Saint Fintan's well-tree came into being when the holy well nearby was profaned and ceased to flow. Water appeared in a crook of the tree into which the spirit of Saint Fintan migrated, and it was recognized with rites and ceremonies appropriate to a holy well.

Two of the major pardons (penitential ceremonies) of East Morbihan in Brittany celebrate miraculous religious images connected with trees. The Pardon of Notre-Dame-de-la-Tronchaye at Rochefort-en-Terre commemorates a black madonna discovered in a hollow tree during the twelfth century. At Josselin, the Pardon of Notre-Dame-du-Roncier reveres "Our Lady of the Bush." The legend of Josselin tells how, by accident, a ploughman discovered an image of Our Lady in a Rose bush. He took the image home, but during the night, like an *Alraun* (mandrake),* it transported itself back again to the bush. After several fruitless journeys, it was decided to make a shrine at the rosebush. It soon gained a reputation for curing people from epilepsy. The revolutionaries burned the image in 1793, but a fragment was retrieved from the ashes by a devotee, and this is enshrined today in a modern chapel on the site of the Rosebush. *Dris*, the Hedge- or Dog-rose is one of the "bushes" recognized by the Brehon Law of Ireland.

Another miraculous Rosebush was the origin of the veneration of Our Lady at the pilgrimage shrine of Ave Maria at Deggingen, south Germany. In the fourteenth century, a thorn-bearing Rosebush of ancient veneration was about to be cut down. But when the woodsman noticed the words "Ave Maria" on each leaf, this was recognized as a divine sign. Instead of cutting down the Rose, it was venerated. Later, a chapel, now called Alt-Ave, was erected by Franciscan monks at the site. A Rose bush grew by the north wall of Alt-Ave until 1996, when the area around the chapel was cleared during renovation work, and it was destroyed. The image of the miraculous plant, formerly painted on the chapel's altar, was covered over with gray paint at the same time.

Dancing Trees and Trained Trees

English folk tradition tells that several ancient buildings were built on living trees. They include the Old Manor House at Knaresborough in Yorkshire, the hall of Huntingfield in Suffolk, and the Cross Keys Inn at Saffron Walden in Essex. In western England, especially near the

---

*In the German tradition, an *Alraun* is a humanoid-shaped root, purchased for the smallest amount, which brings good fortune to the owner at first. However, it soon becomes a burden and all attempts to destroy it are thwarted. If it is taken far from home and left somewhere, it will be back at home when the owner returns. Symbolically, the Alraun stands for something that at first appears a wondrous help but soon becomes a liability.

Devon-Cornwall border, it was the custom to alter certain trees as they grew. In his *A Book of Devon*, S. Baring-Gould described one of them, the Cross Tree at Moreton Hampstead (1909, 226–27):

> The tree is an elm, and it grows out of the basement of the old village cross, the lower steps of which engirdle the trunk. . . . The Elm, grown to a considerable size, was pollarded and had its branches curiously trained, so that the upper portion was given the shape of a table. On this tree-top it was customary on certain occasions to lay a platform, railed round, access to which was obtained by a ladder, and on this tree-top dancing took place.

Baring-Gould quotes entries from a local journal that tell how the "Dancing Tree" was used (1909, 227):

> August 28th, 1801.—The Cross Tree floored and seated round, with a platform, railed on each side, from the top of an adjoining garden wall to the tree, and a flight of steps in the garden for the company to ascend. After passing the platform they enter under a grand arch formed of boughs. There is sufficient room for thirty persons to sit around, and six couples to dance, besides the orchestra. From the novelty of this rural apartment it is expected much company will resort there during the summer.

Sadly, the Moreton Hampstead Cross Tree was destroyed in a gale on October 1, 1891.

Other places in Devon also had "dancing trees." Baring-Gould writes (1909, 228): "On the high road from Exeter to Okehampton, near Dunsford, is a similar tree, but an oak, and this was woven and extended and fashioned into a flat surface." According to local lore, the Fulford family of Great Fulford, held their lands on condition that they should dine once a year on top of this Oak, and hold a dance there for their tenants. Another such tree, the "Meavy Oak," grew near to the village

According to contemporary Druidic teachings, the trilithon signifies the three consonantal groups of Oghams, with the ground between the stones representing the vowels.

of Lifton on the road from Okehampton to Launceston. Said to be the earliest tree to put forth leaves in springtime, it was next to an inn called *The Royal Oak*. During festivities, the Meavy Oak, otherwise the Gospel Oak, supported a platform augmented by pillars. There was yet another similar Oak at Trebursye, near Launceston, in Cornwall. It was said to be haunted by the ghost of a woman who had fallen from it during a dance and perished.

Holy trees were important places of worship in the elder faith, and the traditions were continued in modified form in the Christian church. Gospel Oaks are places where religious services are or were held at certain times of year. Until the nineteenth century, marriages were conducted beneath an Oak at Brampton in Cumbria. Earlier Maytide customs all over Merry England saw many a "greenwood marriage" (or "Mad-Merry Marriage") conducted at such trees without Christian clergy being present. A service is held annually at Old Polstead Gospel Oak in Suffolk, and the practice continues in many other places, particularly in south Germany, where outdoor services are conducted at notable Oaks on Whitsunday.

In mainland Europe, trees, especially Lindens (Lime trees, *Tilia platyphyllos*), were altered to take the form of a series of circular platforms, one above the other. Their shape reproduced the traditional "cosmic axis," where the different planes of spiritual existence are "stacked" one on top of the other (as taught in Bardic tradition). Such trees are recorded as far back as the year 1200, where, in his Arthurian epic *Parzival*, Wolfram von Eschenbach gives the account of how Sigune sits weeping in the crown of a Linden with the corpse of her lover. Dating from around 1501 in Queen Anne of Brittany's *Book of Hours* is an illuminated page by Jean Bourdichon that shows a Maying scene. Two youths are coming out of woodland carry flowering "May Branches." Nearby grows a three-tiered tree, on which hang suspended eggs and apples. John Speed's map of the town of Flint, in north Wales (1610), shows one, along with a Maypole and stocks in the central square outside the church. Living examples have survived into modern times in the Netherlands and parts of Germany, and although most have disappeared, there are a number of new ones growing today.

6
Welsh Bardic Scripts

Three things which a Bard ought to make with his own hands:
his Coelbren, his Roll and his Plagawd.

BARDIC TRIAD FROM THE
BARDDAS OF IOLO MORGANWG [EDWARD WILLIAMS]

A BRIEF OVERVIEW OF BARDIC SCRIPTS

The entire body of ancient Celtic lore and legend was transmitted from mouth to ear, without being written down. The oldest written texts contain material that may have existed in oral form for centuries before being committed to writing. Most ancient written sources contain legends, history, genealogies, and tales of the gods. From written sources alone, it is reasonable to assert that Bardo-Druidic tradition has a continuity from at least the sixth century CE.

The secret and initiated traditions, jealously guarded, were not consigned to writing until much later, if at all. Also, the vagaries of history have meant that what comes down to us from ancient times must, of necessity, be but a fragment of what has existed over time. It is clear that many, if not most, texts have come into being and passed away without trace. Only when copies have been made, have texts survived—and then sometimes, only fragmentarily. In addition,

The eternal flow of the waters, put into symbolic form by the fountain,
signifies the cyclic nature of events that is implicit
in Bardo-Druidic spirituality.

transcribers and collators often added material where it was lacking, or corrected what they believed to be wrong.

Historically, however, none of this can be verified. The material emerged into the public domain during the Celtic Revival of the eighteenth century when Druidism and Bardism were of great interest in Welsh, Scottish, and Irish literary circles. The bestseller poems "Fingal" (1761) and "Temora" (1763), which were presented as the rediscovered ancient writings of a Bard named Ossian, triggered off a penchant for ancient Celtic literature and lore—real and otherwise. In reality, Ossian had been concocted by the Scottish poet James MacPherson (1736–1796), and the hoax was soon exposed.

Nevertheless, the desire for such romantic Celtiana did not fade away. In London in 1781, Henry Hurle (1739–1795) created a mystical order on Masonic lines called the Ancient Order of Druids (AOD). A mythos was written for the intitation ritual concerning a love affair during the first-century CE Roman Conquest of Britain. It was between a British Bard called Tacitus Magallas and a princess named Sensitoria Roxiana. The Bard was slain resisting the Romans, and the princess gave birth to a baby named Togo Dubellinus, whom she reared in a sequestered forest. Druids out cutting mistletoe found the baby concealed in a hollow oak tree and brought him up. In adulthood he became the greatest of Archdruids. Numerous other Druidic orders emerged in the nineteeth century, but the AOD still exists at the time of writing. A sigil combining the Greek letters Tau and Delta, signifying Togo Dubellinus, is one of the emblems of this order. Oak leaves and acorns, mistletoe and long-handed sickles (used for cutting it), standing stones, Stonehenge, and the Bardic harp are other emblems that were adopted by many Druidic orders that split from the AOD or formed in other ways. But neither Ogham nor Coelbren appeared in the regalia of these groups.

In this heady milieu, the Welsh stonemason Edward Williams (1747–1826)—who wrote under his Bardic name Iolo Morganwg, according to the "privilege and usage of the Bards of the Isle of

Britain" (Williams Ab Ithel 1874, II:165)—is the prime example of this Romantic impulse. He was a key figure in the history of both the Welsh Eisteddfod, which he re-established in his first Gorsedd in London in 1792,* and in the development of modern Celtic spirituality, including contemporary Druidry. Over many years, Iolo claimed, he had collected together, compiled, edited, and added to texts that he had received both orally and in manuscript from other preservers of Welsh culture. Scholarly commentators noted that much of his material, the *Iolo Manuscripts* and other texts, had never been seen or published before, and it was recognized that he must have written most of it himself (see Constantine 2007). It was in these texts that Iolo restated or created the Bardic knowledge that underlies contemporary Druidic teachings. It was a theistic creed, which even though a product of Iolo's personal vision, was available as a coherent system that was subsequently found to be of spiritual value. The Druids were not seen as Pagan, but as early deists. On a "pilgrimage" to Stonehenge in 1867, having gone there on a special train from Bristol to Salisbury, assembled members of the Ancient Order of Druids were led into the circle by Brother Yeates "bearing an open Bible" (*The Western Daily Press*, 30 July 1867, p. 3).

The promoters of the Welsh National Eisteddfod at Llangollen in 1858 "offered a prize of £30, and a Bardic tiara in gold, for the 'fullest illustration from original sources of the theology, discipline, and usages

---

*At the end of the eighteenth century, Iolo was one of the two members of the "Bardic Institution," the other being the Reverend Edward Evan of Aberdare. The Eisteddfod organized by Iolo in 1792, which is the direct forerunner of the contemporary Welsh *eisteddfodau* (pl.), was convened on Primrose Hill near London (now part of Regent's Park) at *alban elfed*, the autumnal equinox. It brought together Welsh and English Bards and Druids in a bilingual (Welsh and English) celebration of British Bardism. A few years later, nationalist Welsh Druids declared that only Welsh was the proper language of Bardism, and the English Bards and Druids were barred from further participation. The concept that the "Red Dragon has two tongues" had not yet emerged. There was thus a split in the Bardic current that Iolo had brought together. Both the Welsh Druids and the English Druids proceeded on their own pathways, which they continue to do today, for, as the Druid Colin Murray remarked to me in 1978: "England is also a Celtic country."

of the Bardo-druidic system in the Isle of Britain'" (Williams Ab Ithel 1862–1874, I:xiii). Only one text was received, which came from an unknown Bard called Plennydd. The Bardic judges of the Eisteddfod, chaired by Myfyr Morganwg, deemed the text authentic:

> The compiler has been very diligent, and remarkably successful in obtaining access to such a vast number of ancient manuscripts bearing on Bardism. . . . With respect to the genuineness, Plennydd justly observes,—"though their authors cannot in many instances be named, any more than we can name the authors of the Common Law of England, yet the existence of the peculiar dogmas and usages which they represent may be proved from the compositions of the Bards from the era of Taliesin down to the present time." (Williams Ab Ithel 1862–1874, I:xiv).

It emerged subsequently that the text was the work of none other than the late Iolo Morganwg himself. His great work was edited by the Reverend John Williams Ab Ithel and published at Llandovery in 1862 under the title *Barddas; or, a Collection of Original Documents, Illustrative of the Theology, Wisdom, and Usages of the Bardo-Druidic System of the Isle of Britain*. A second volume of material was issued in 1874. Later academics who examined *Barddas* claimed that they could not find any of Iolo's sources, and thus, his work must be a forgery (in their understanding of textual authenticity). However, the Bardic judges of 1858 had already taken this into account, and dismissed the possibility. But, whatever their origin, since then, the teachings in *Barddas* have existed in their own right, and have had a massive influence on the development of Druidry. "Morganwgian Druidry" has existed now for over two centuries and has always been the significant element in the British Druidic movement.

According to Iolo's account, the principal collator of ancient Welsh writings was the sixteenth-century Bard Llewellyn Sion of Llangewydd. When he was young, Llewellyn Sion was a student of the Bards Thomas

Llewelyn of Rhegoes and of Meurig Davydd of Llanisan. Both of these men were eminent Bards of the Glamorgan Chair. Llewellyn Sion was a worthy successor, gaining recognition as a composer of elegant verse. His fame as a Bard gained him employment making and selling transcripts of collectable Welsh manuscripts. His work brought him into contact with eminent collectors of ancient Welsh manuscripts, to which he was given free access. Llewellyn Sion was thus enabled to make copies, so preserving many texts that otherwise might have been destroyed. For instance, Sir William Herbert invited Llewellyn Sion to Rhaglan Castle to study his major collection of manuscripts. Later, it was completely destroyed by fire during Cromwell's civil war.

In 1560 Llewellyn Sion took over the honor of presiding in the Bardic Chair of Glamorgan. He wrote a book that collated together much of the information he had gleaned from the ancient texts. Titled *Atgofion Gwybodau yr Hen Gymry*, by all accounts it was a major treatise on ancient Welsh traditional knowledge. How much of it was doctored by or actually written by Iolo is uncertain. It dealt with classical Welsh poetry, genealogy, memorials, agriculture, customary law, medicine, chemistry, and handicrafts. Unfortunately, it was never published. The story was that the manuscript was sent to London for publication. But during preparation, Llewellyn Sion died at an advanced age, and for some reason the book never appeared. However, Iolo tells us, parts of the work survived in some form or another until the eighteenth century, when they were collated by Welsh Bardic scholars, including Iolo himself. It is from them—or, most likely, Iolo—that we have our present knowledge of the *Coelbren y Beirdd*, the Welsh Bardic "alphabets."

In contrast to ancient Celtic Ogham and the Germanic runes, which have a genuine provenance and literature from antiquity, the historic nature of Coelbren is questionable (Constantine 2007, 105–11). In promoting a supposedly ancient secret alphabet, Iolo may have been influenced by the medieval magical alphabets that appeared in Francis Barrett's 1801 book *The Magus, or Celestial Intelligencer*. The Masonic

The Tablets of the Bards, with Llawdden's 37-character
Coelbren y Beirdd, according to Iolo Morganwg.

lodges of that era also had their secret ciphers. The Bardic Alphabet has never been used much, and the various Druid groups of the nineteeth century seem to have ignored it. It appeared in a Scottish context in the *Leabhar Comunn nam Fior Ghael—The Book of the Club of True Highlanders* along with runes, the Gaelic alphabet, and Ogham (North 1881, 1:pl. XIV); and in Dudley Wright's *The Ancient Faith of Britain*, where he claims that the Bardic Coelbren was derived from the Etruscan script (1924, 29–30). In recent years, Coelbren has appeared on at least one Ogham divination card deck.

Divine Origins

According to the tradition, the characters of the *Coelbren y Beirdd* are derived from the basic structure of existence, brought into the world of humans through mystic revelation. Bardo-Druidic teachings state that the origin of letters was simultaneous with the creation of the universe. They are a manifestation of a primal vibration, which, according to Celtic Christian mysticism, is the Word of God. This tradition is explained in *Barddas* as follows:

> When God pronounced His name, with the word sprang the light and the life; for previously there was no life except God Himself. And the mode in which it was spoken was of God's direction. His name was pronounced, and with the utterance was the springing of light and vitality, and man, and every other living thing; that is to say, each and all sprang together. (Williams Ab Ithel 1862–1874, I:17)

From the light, which Bardo-Druidry deems the most perfect manifestation of the divine, came the revelation of the concept of writing:

> Menw the Aged, son of Menwyd, beheld the springing of the light, and its form and appearance . . . in three columns; and in the rays of light, the vocalization—for one were the hearing and seeing, one in unison with the form and sound was life, and one unitedly with

these three was power, which power was God the Father. And by seeing the form, and in it hearing the voice—not otherwise—he knew what form and appearance voice should have. . . . And it was on hearing the sound of the voice, which had in it the kind and utterance of three notes, that he obtained the three letters, and knew the sign that was suitable to one and other of them. Thus he made in form and sign the Name of God, after the semblance of rays of light, and perceived that they were the figure and form and sign of life. . . .

It was from the understanding thus obtained in respect of this voice, that he was able to assimilate mutually every other voice as to kind, quality and reason, and could make a letter suitable to the utterance of every sound and voice. Thus were obtained the Cymraeg (Welsh), and every other language. (Williams 1862–1874, I:17–19)

This Bardo-Druidic "creation myth" differs from other European myths of the same kind in that it does not describe the making of matter by a supernatural Demiurge or Creator, but the springing of human awareness of it. To the Bards, "creation" is the "springing of the light," the moment when the human witness who beholds the divine act gains conscious awareness of existence. Creation is the arrival of consciousness, that moment at which everything that exists could now be seen and described. This sacred story recognizes the interrelatedness and essential oneness of all things in existence, as defined by consciousness. The definition of existence by the "utterance of every sound and voice" was the foundation of transmittable human culture, the beginning of history, for word and symbol enable the past to be recalled, the present to be defined and transmitted into times yet to come.

The Holy Name of God, from which all things were held to emanate, was rarely spoken by monotheistic Druids or Celtic Christians out of respect and for fear of the consequences of taking a holy name "in vain":

It is considered presumptuous to utter this name in the hearing of any man in the world. Nevertheless, every thing calls him inwardly by this name—the sea and land, earth and air, and all the visibles and invisibles of the world, whether on the earth or in the sky—all the worlds of all of the celestials and the terrestrials—every intellectual being and existence. (Williams Ab Ithel 1862–1874, I:23)

The Welsh name of God was symbolized by the *Awen*. This is the primary Bardic and Druidic sigil, written as three lines radiating from above. *Barddas* recounts how each of the three lines of the Awen have a specific meaning:

Thus are they made—the first of the signs is a small cutting or line inclining with the sun at eventide, thus / ; the second is another cutting, in the form of a perpendicular, upright post, | ; and the third is a cutting of the same amount of inclination as the first, but in an opposite direction, that is, against the sun, thus \ and the three placed together, thus /|\. (Williams Ab Ithel 1862–1874, I:21)

Together, the Awen represents conscious awareness, symbolically the threefold or triadic nature of existence. Past, present and future can only be recognized by conscious beings.

The Awen also has an alphabetic form—OIV. Its Bardo-Druidic explanation is that O was given in the first column of light, I to the second or middle light-column, and V to the third. *Barddas* recounts:

It was by means of this word that God declared His existence, life, knowledge, power, eternity, and universality. And in the declaration was his love, that is coinstantaneously with it sprung like lightning all the universe into life and existence, co-vocally and co-jubilantly with the uttered Name of God, in one united song of exultation and joy—then all the worlds to the extremities of Annwn. (Williams Ab Ithel 1862–1874, I:19)

PRACTICAL DEVELOPMENTS

Although these letters were divine in origin, they were insufficient for writing useful texts. The invention of Welsh writing proper is attributed to Einigan Gawr (Einigan the Giant). Legend tells how Einigan invented writing to preserve the memory of the life of his father, Huon, son of Alser. He seems to have made the invention in mainland Europe, for Llewellyn Sion tells how: "He came to his father's kindred in the Isle of Britain, and exhibited his art, and they adjudged him to be the wisest of the wise and called him Einigan the Gwyddon [Einigan the Wise]." (Williams Ab Ithel 1862–1874, I:53) Einigan's record was made by carving letters into wood (the old word *pren*). Both the letters and the tablets on which they were written were called Coelbren, the "Wood of credibility."

Like the Ogham and Runic scripts, Coelbren is composed of angular letters designed to be cut easily in wood or stone. In *Barddas*, the section on *"Awgrym"* (Symbol) tells us:

> The best wood in respect to the facility of chipping and grooving is hazel wood, . . . or willow wood, ... The best of all willows is the yellow willow. The ancient Poets, however, sought the mountain ash [Rowan], regarding it as charmed wood, because worms will not devour or corrupt it, and because no vain spirit, or wicked fiend, will abide where there is mountain ash, and because neither charm nor enchantment can avail against mountain ash, nor injure it, nor him who carries it, because no deadly poison can touch them. (Williams Ab Ithel 1862–1874, I:19)

According to the *Barddas* concerning *"Cyfrinach y Beirdd—Lluniad Llythyrenau"* (The Bardic Secret—Formation of Letters), the original letters were very simple, being derived from the three basic forms of the Awen. Bardic lore tells how the ancient Celts had only ten characters in their letter-row before they migrated to Britain. This story concurs with the legend of Einigan Gawr, who devised writing in mainland Europe. This continental Celtic alphabet may have been derived from Greek, which was used by certain Gallic Druids for inscriptions and calendars. It seems to have been a Bardic secret, for, even after the Coelbren was devised, these ten characters were revered as special. The earliest form of British Coelbren comprised sixteen characters, in the form of rays of light. Individual Bardic characters they called *llythyrau* (sg. *llythyr*), which, according to Iolo, derives from *lly*, meaning what is "manifold," "various," or "manifest," and *tyr*, "to cut" (Williams Ab Ithel 1862–1874, I:24 n.1).* Another name for the letter-row is *Abcedilros*, from the letter-order. Later Bardo-Druidic interpretations saw these letters, derived from the Awen, as a synesthetic experience: "Accordingly the memory of seeing could thus take place simultaneously with the memory of hearing; and, by means of signs, every sound of voice could be rendered visible to the eye" (Williams Ab Ithel 1862–1874, I:23).

According to this legendary history, the sixteen-character Coelbren was devised during the reign of the British king Dyfnwal Moelmud ap Dyfnvarth ap Prydain ap Aeth Mawr. He is better known as the lawgiver Dunvallo Molmutius, who, according to Geoffrey of Monmouth's *Historia Regum Britanniae* (ca. 1136), reigned 430–390 BCE. Later, in the reign of Beli Mawr ap Manog (King Beli the Great, son of Manogan), the secret of this sixteen-character "alphabet" was "divulged" to noninitiates. Then, each letter was revised, and given a new, public, form. Because the secret was out, it was announced that forthwith there should be no king, judge, or teacher in the country who could not read and understand the esoteric meanings of this alphabet.

Once the "alphabet" was in general use, sixteen characters proved insufficient. Two further characters were added before the time of

---

*The etymology is fanciful, as Middle Welsh *llythyr* is more simply explained as a borrowing of Latin *littera*, "letter."

Taliesin (sixth century CE). At this period, with the introduction of the Christian religion, the cipher OIV came into use as the Name of God. According to one account, Taliesin enlarged the alphabet by adding a further two characters: "The language of twenty letters is in Awen," he wrote (Williams Ab Ithel 1862–1874, I:67). However, the introduction of the twenty-character Coelbren is also ascribed to Ithel Felyn (Ithel the Tawny). Bardo-Druidic lore teaches that this version of Coelbren continued in use until the knowledge and use of Latin as an everyday language ceased in Britain. It is notable that the earliest and most widespread version of Ogham also had twenty "characters."

Geraint Fardd Glas (Geraint the Blue Bard, who flourished around 900 CE) is credited with enlarging the character-set further by adding four "auxiliary symbols." These resemble the five forfeadha of Ogham. This new Coelbren of twenty-four characters was used by Bards for "black and white" (writing in ink) until the late Middle Ages. It was this version that the Bards employed for secret communication among themselves. It also appeared in the form of dice, used for divination. The Bardic tradition tells of the *Five Ages of Letters*. The first of these was the age of three letters, when the Awen, representing the godhead, was taken as the basis of writing. The second age of letters used sixteen characters. The third age began when two further letters were added, making eighteen, and the fourth age used twenty-four characters. Finally, in the fifth age, the final development of Coelbren expanded it to thirty-eight characters. This was described by the Bard Ieuan Llawdden, Rector of Machynlleth, who flourished around 1440 to 1480. This long character set had a limited function, being used only for carving on wood. The twenty-four-character row remained the standard form.

THE BARDS' WOOD IN LANGUAGE AND METAPHOR

The importance of wood-lore is very significant in the worldview of the Celtic Revival. In Welsh, many words concerning consciousness, wisdom,

Menw the Aged, son of Menwyd (Menw hen ap Menw), witnessing the
springing of the light symbolizing the vital instant when human beings gained
conscious awareness of existence, as told in a symbolic tale by Iolo Morganwg.

or learning contain the element *wydd*, which Iolo and some other modern Celtic mystics interpreted as meaning "wood."* Such terms include *arwydd*, a "sign"; *cyfarwydd*, "skillful"; *cyfarwyddyd*, "information"; *cywydd*, a "revelation"; *dedwydd*, "having received knowledge"; *derwydd*, a "Druid"; *egwyddawr*, an "alphabet"; *gwyddon*, a "wise man"; and *gwynwyddigion*, "men of sacred knowledge." (Williams Ab Ithel 1862–1874, I:13)

According to the *Barddas* materials, the Welsh Bards in particular have long used the metaphor of "wood" to describe words, especially poetry. The twelfth-century Bard Rhys Gach ab Riccert (1140–1170) wrote:

> *The wooden axe of an unpolished bard,*
> *Has been hewing a song to Gwenllian.*
> (WILLIAMS AB ITHEL 1862–1874, I:11)

Another famous Bard, Iolo Goch (1315–1402), stated:

> *I will bear for Owain,*
> *In metrical words, fresh and slow,*
> *Continually, not the hewing of alder wood,*
> *By the chief carpenter of song.*
> (AB ITHEL 1862–1874, I:12)

The poet Dafydd ab Gwilym (1340–1368) said "This will address them on wood," while Rhys Goch Eryri (1330–1420) wrote: "No longer will be seen the mark of the axe / Of the flower of the carpenters on a song-loving and wise one"; and Ieuan du'r Bilwg (1460–1500): "May thy praise go—thou art a soldier— / Upon wood, as long as day and

---

*This etymological connection is fanciful: the *wydd* in most of these terms does not refer to "wood" but rather to "knowledge" (from the Indo-European root that is cognate with English "wit"). The word *egwyddawr* (properly *egwyddor*, from Middle Welsh *egwyðawr*) has a different source: it is a Welshified borrowing of Latin *abecedarium*.

water continue" (Williams Ab Ithel 1862–1874, I:12).* In 1530, Harri ap Rhys Gwilym spoke of "The degrees and Roll of wood-knowledge, / The root of sciences, for the weaving of a song of praise" (Williams Ab Ithel 1862–1874, I:14).*

ALTERNATIVE FORMS: PYROGRAPHY, STONE, AND PLAGAWD

In addition to carving Coelbren characters onto wood, the Bards developed a system of pyrography using hot iron stamps. This technique may have been developed from coin dies or the stamps and moulds used in pottery. If it is as ancient as Bardic tradition makes it, then it may be the first example of "movable type" printing in the world. Legendary history dates it from before the Roman occupation of Britain (43–410 CE):

> It was in the time of Llyr of Defective Speech that the way of burning the cyrvens with an iron stamp was understood, that is, there was an iron for every letter, heated red hot, with which they burnt on an ebill or a board what was required; and sometimes they formed letters on wood with the small prickings of a hot fork. (Williams Ab Ithel 1862–1874, I:155)

Although no indisputable ancient inscriptions exist in the Bardic Abcedilros, in cases where they written on slate or carved in stone, they are called *Coelvain*, and the stones on which they are carved, *Peithynvain* (sg. *Peithynvaen*), the "stones of elucidation." "They wrote with a steel pencil on both surfaces of the stones, and then put them on a strong cord, or on an iron or brass rod, which passed through the top of every

---

*The dates given here for these poets all derive from Iolo and are often problematic in the light of better historical information; the alleged texts and their translations are likely to also contain problems in part or in whole, considering the source. The "carpenters of song" metaphor is nevertheless genuine (see Suggett 2006–2007, 251–52; Davies 1995).

Peithynvaen" (Williams Ab Ithel 1862–1874, I:159). This infers that the "stones" were flat slates. In the tenth century CE, Blegywryd, Archdeacon of Llandaff and the clerk of King Howel the Good (Hywel Dda)

> faced the hall of the prince's court with stones, one side and another of the hall, and on the stones wrote in order, with a strong pencil, the laws which Howel imposed upon the country and nation of the Cymry [Wales], an open entrance being left for every man that needed . . . whether a native or a stranger, to proceed into the hall, and to read the law, or to have it read to him. Hence it became customary to inscribe a vocal song, a Roll, a poem, the memorial of praiseworthy deeds, and the narration of wisdom, on Peithynvain, and to place them on the face of walls and partitions, or on strings, or iron rods. (Williams Ab Ithel 1862–1874, I:159–61)

King Arthur is said to have had the "system of the Round Table," and the praiseworthy deeds of its knights, written on plates of brass and tin. They were displayed in his three principal courts, at Caerleon-upon-Usk, Cellwig (Pendennis Castle), and Penrhyn Rhionydd (Glasgow). In former times at Caernarfon was the "stone of enigmas," the tomb-slab of the ancient Welsh astronomer Gwydon ap Don. It was carved with letters only intelligible to the Bards. Secret Coelvains were also made in stone. They were comparable with the "Charms of the Bards" (*Barddrin*), small stones bearing Bardic characters, which were arranged appropriately to convey information. Sometimes, these messages were encrypted further to minimize the chances of unwelcome readers.

Although wood was always the medium of choice for Bardic poetry, other writing materials became available in Britain during the Roman occupation (44–410 CE). Bardic tradition tells how Bendigeidfran, father of the famed Celtic king Caradog (Caractacus), brought the technique of writing on parchment scrolls to Britain. Bendigeidfran learnt the technique during his seven years' captivity in Rome as a hostage on behalf of his son. On his return to Britain, he taught the indigenous

Traditional cosmological symbolism is embedded within the forms of
ancient Celtic art, most explicitly in sacred structures such a cauldrons,
shrines, croziers, healing-stones, reliquaries, and crosses.

scribes how to prepare goat skins for parchment. Although it was more convenient than wood, the more conservative Bards would not use the new technique. This refusal by the Bards to change their materials led to their writings being called *Coelbren y Beirdd*, literally, the "wood-script of the Bards," as contrasted with Latin writings on parchment.

Bardo-Druidic history tells that paper was invented by a citizen of Constantinople called Moran. He devised a technique of grinding up flax and spreading it out thinly to make sheets of paper. Like parchment, flax paper was also used in Britain. But it was always considered inferior to another writing material, *Plagawd*:

> Plagawd was a plant of the lily kind, which was brought over from India; and on it they wrote with black, or some other colour. After that, Plagawd of skin was made, being manufactured by art. (Williams Ab Ithel 1862–1874, I:163)

According to some accounts, Plagawd originated in Egypt, not India, so it may have been Papyrus. Once Plagawd was imported, we are told, writing on trees was marginalized. Only the Bards maintained the tradition, out of an inner understanding that the medium is significant. In medieval times, only a few of them continued the tradition, and most Bards wrote in ink on parchment or paper.

THE RETURN OF "WOOD WISDOM"

Iolo relates that (according to Llewellyn Sion) after the defeat in 1400 of the uprising led by the Welsh nobleman Owain Glyndwr (1349–1415), the Lancastrian king of England, Henry IV, forbade the importation of paper or Plagawd into Wales, and its manufacture there. He did this to prevent learning and written communication between Welsh people, or with foreigners. In addition, Bards were forbidden to travel around their normal circuits, or to make official visits to families, as in former times. However, this attempt to extirpate Welsh culture was counterproductive, for its consequence was the reinstatement of the use of the Coelbren of the Bards of the Isle of Britain. According to Welsh commentators, persecution of Welsh culture by the king of England actually encouraged the reinstatement of the ancient letters.

According to nineteenth-century Welsh Bards, the construction of Coelbrens was seen as an act of cultural resistance against the English-speaking ruling class:

> After recovering the knowledge of the Coelbrens, that is, the one of the Bards and the one of the Monks, nearly every person, male and female, wished to learn and construct them. From thence they became the trade of sieve-makers and basket-makers, and upon them was cut the record of every thing that required the preserved memorial of letter and book. And thus it was until the time of Henry the Seventh, who, being a Cymro [Welshman], took his countrymen under the protection of his courtesy, and placed them, at his own expense, under the instruction of monks, and furnished them gratuitously with as much paper and parchment as was required; and they were taught whatever they would of the two languages, Welsh or English, and many learned both. On that account the knowledge of letters was more frequent among the common people of Wales than it was in England. (Williams Ab Ithel 1862–1874, I:139–41)

Making and Using Bardic Frames

The making of Bardic Frames was described by Llewelyn Sion:

> They gathered rods of hazel or mountain ash [rowan] in the winter, about a cubit in length, and split each into four parts, that is, the wood was made into four splinters, and kept them, until by the working of time they became quite dry. Then they planed them square, in respect of breadth and thickness, and afterwards

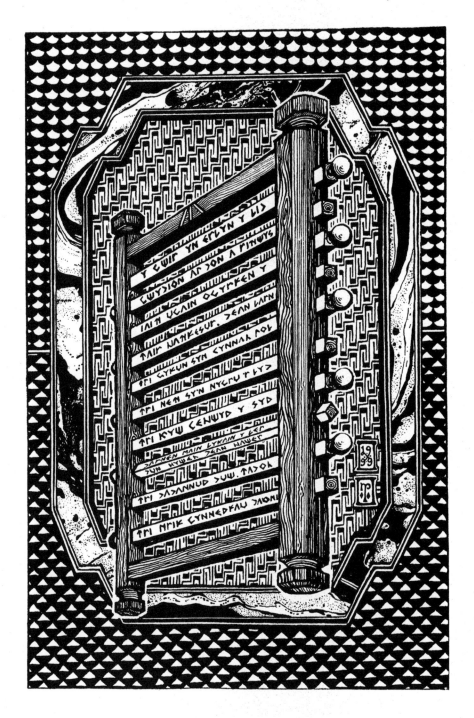

Peithenyn, the Bardic Frame, according to *Barddas*.

trimmed down the angles to the tenth part of an inch, which was done [in order] that the cuttings of the letters, that is, the symbols, which were cut with the knife on one of the four square surfaces, should not encroach visibly upon the next face; and thus on every one of the four faces. Then they cut the symbols, according to their character, whether they were those of language and speech, or of numbers, or other signs of art, such as the symbols of music, of voice, and string. And after cutting ten such bars as were required, they prepared four splinters, two and two, which were called *pill*, planed them smooth, placed two of them together side by side across the frame, and marked the places for ten holes. After that, they cut the holes, that is, half of each of the ten holes, in one splinter, and the same in the other; and they did the same with the other two splinters; and these are called *pillwydd*. Then they took the symbolized or lettered bars, and made a neck at each of the two ends of every bar, all round, the breadth of a finger, along the bar. Then they placed the lettered sticks by their necks on one of the pillwydd at one end, and in like manner at the other end; and on that the other pillwydd at each end, hole for hole. And on both ends of the two pillwydden they made necks, as places for strings to tie them firmly together at each end of the symbolized sticks. And when the whole are thus bound tight together, the book that is constructed in this manner is called *Peithynen*, because it is framed; the pillwydd at each end keeping all together, and the ebillion, or lettered staves, turning freely in the pillwydd, and thus being easy to read. That is, one face of the ebill is read first, according to the number of its face, then it is turned with the sun, and the second face is read, and it is turned so for every other face, and thus from ebill to ebill until the reading is finished. A number from one to ten being on the turning face of each of the ebillion, the numbered face is the first that is to be read, and then the others in the order of their course with the sun.

There are forty sides to the ebillion in every Peithynen; after that, another Peithynen is formed, until the conclusion of the poem or narrative. And where than more than ten ebillion are required, and less than a score, as many ebillion as are required are placed altogether in one entire Peithenyn. The reason for assigning ten as the particular number of succession, is, that ten is the division point of number, and under the number of decades are all numbers arranged, until language cannot give them names. (Williams Ab Ithel 1862–1874, I:135–37)

Regarding the type of wood, we are informed:

The best wood wherewith to construct a Peithenyn are young oak saplings, as thick as would leave the ebillion large enough, after the tree has been split into four parts, and the rind and epidermis completely chipped off from each quarter. They should be well dried before they are finished and lettered: the best time to cut the wood is the Feast of St. Mary. (Williams Ab Ithel 1862–1874, I:149)

OTHER SECRET SYSTEMS

Because Coelbren was divulged to the common people after being kept secret for centuries, in addition to the Peithenyn, the Bards developed other clandestine means of communication. Very small ebillion were employed for intimate nonverbal communication by initiates. They were "a finger long," and had notches "so that they may be used by two persons or more, who are confidants. It is by placing and joining them together . . . that words and phrases are formed; . . . they are called the Charms of the Bards, or Bardic Mystery" (Williams Ab Ithel 1862–1874, I:155). The Bards used these charms to create words for others to read. They also had a use in divination, a function that was facilitated by another variant, the "Coelbren of Simple Characters."

The Coelbren of Simple Characters consists of individual pieces of wood, usually cubic in form, with single Coelbren characters on each face. A common version used a set of four cubic dice, with one face for each of the twenty-four characters:

> Every one of the pieces was four sided, having six surfaces to each, and a letter on each surface, differently coloured, so that what was wanted might be obtained at first sight without much searching. The arrangement of twenty-four was found to be the best for those Coelbrens; and for obtaining mutual knowledge by means of the said Coelbrens secrets were ascertained, which caused much astonishment as to how it was possible. (Williams Ab Ithel 1862–1874, I:155)

Another name for this is the *Palm Coelbren*, defined as:

> that where twenty-four are cut on small dice, that is inasmuch as each die has six sides, and a letter on each side, there will be on the four dice twenty-four letters, besides what may be obtained otherwise, when the die is reversed, in order to show a different letter. . . . By holding some of these in the palm of the hand, and putting them together in the presence of a man of secrecy, dumb conversation can be carried on. (Williams Ab Ithel Ab Ithel 1862–1874, I:157)

Postscript

Through Woods to Wisdom

It is not the intention of the writer to detail the methods of divination that may be applied to the Ogham and Coelbren systems. Since the 1980s, when Liz and Colin Murray published the *Celtic Tree Oracle* card deck (Rider, 1988; republished by Orange Hippo!, 2021) and the 1990s with Nigel Pennick's *The Celtic Oracle: The Ancient Art of the Druids* (Aquarian/Thorsons 1992, with cards by Nigel Jackson),* there has been a burgeoning output of Ogham divination card decks. One online download of oracle cards available in the early 2020s had both Ogham and Coelbren together (MorganaMagicSpell), and there were numerous other hardcopy divination card decks with titles such as *The Ogham Oracle, The Celtic Ogham Alphabet, Celtic Oracle Cards,* and so on. Although an early set of *Koelbren Cards* was published in the mid-1980s by Kaledon Naddair (Inner Keltia, 1984–1986), the use of the Welsh Bardic alphabets as a divination system is more problematical because the individual letters are not specifically tied to a descriptive system like the trees of the Ogham.†
Divination with the Gaelic aibítir is related closely to the Ogham methods.

---

*An expanded text without cards was published as *The New Celtic Oracle* (Capall Bann, 1997).

†In his book *The Coelbren Alphabet* (2017; rev. ed.: *Coelbren*, 2023), John Michael Greer posits that it is based primarily on a Welsh phonetic system rather than meanings of characters. Greer's book is the only study to date that presents a substantial discussion of Coelbren as a divinatory tool.

The mythological figure of Étaín, whose radiant beauty stirred the
underworldly Midir to woo her as his second wife.

If we believe in the philosophical idea of perfection, then we must recognize that all systems that attempt to arrange and describe the complexity of existence must fall short of this goal. However carefully it may be arranged, every description is flawed, because it is impossible to stand outside the continuous flux of events. As a traditional Scots Gaelic adage states:

Ri traghad
'S ri lionadh . . .
Mar a bha
Mar a tha
Mar a bhitheas
Gu brath
Ri tragadh
'S ri lionadh.

An English translation is:

Ebbing and flowing . . .
As it was,
As it is,
As it shall be, evermore—
The ebb and the flow.

(SHARP 1920, 103)

Although they are necessary for everyday life to continue, all systems of classification must in some degree fail. There is a narrow line between using a system while recognizing its arbitrary nature and taking it literally as a true description of reality, which is essentially only able to be experienced at first hand. This is understood in Bardo-Druidic teachings, whose flexibility allows them to be practiced in ways appropriate to any conditions that we may encounter.

All spiritual traditions are founded on a specific framework cognitive of one kind or another. People who possess a cognitive framework for their knowledge of existence on all its levels have a better chance of achieving their potential than those who have a chaotic worldview, for then they are chaotic within themselves. The nature of the Bardo-Druidic cognitive framework is expressed innately through the systems I describe in this book. Through them it is possible to gain access to the essentials of the inner wisdom of the Bardo-Druidic system of the British Isles, and to thereby to live creatively.

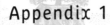

Appendix 1

Ogham Correspondences

The tables below present the most commonly recognized Ogham correspondences. Bird Ogham only applies to the first twenty feadha.

THE AICME OF *BEITH* (B, L, F, S, N)

Name	Roman letter	Tree	Name	Bird	Color
Beith	B	Birch	*Besan*	Pheasant	White
Luis	L	Rowan	*Lachu*	Duck	Gray
Fearn	F	Alder	*Faelinn*	Gull	Crimson
Saille	S	Willow	*Seg*	Hawk	Bright (beautiful)
Nuin	N	Ash	*Naescu*	Snipe	Clear

THE AICME OF *HUATH* (H, D, T, C, Q)

Name	Roman letter	Tree	Name	Bird	Color
Huath	H	Hawthorn	*Hadaig*	Crow	"Terrible" (Purple)
Duir	D	Oak	*Droem*	Wren	Black
Tinne	T	Holly	*Truith*	Starling	Gray-green
Coll	C	Hazel	*Corr*	Crane	Brown
Quert	Q	Apple	*Querc*	Chicken	Green

THE AICME OF *MUIN* (M, G, NG, ST, R)

Name	Roman letter	Tree	Name	Bird	Color
Muin	M	Vine	Mintan	Titmouse	Multi-colored
Gort	G	Ivy	Géis	Mute	Swan-blue
Ngetal	Ng	Reed	Ngéigh	Goose	Yellowish Green
Straif	St	Blackthorn	Stmolach	Thrush	Purple-black
Ruis	R	Elder	Rócnat	Rook	Blood-red

THE AICME OF *AILM* (A, O, U, E, I)

Name	Roman letter	Tree	Name	Bird	Color
Ailm	A	Elm (Fir)	Aidhircléog	Lapwing	Black-white
On	O	Furze	Odorscrach	Cormorant	Dun
Ur	U	Heather	Uiséog	Lark	Purple
Edadh	E	Aspen	Ela	Swan	Fox-red
Ida	I	Yew	Illait	Eaglet	White

THE FORFEADHA OR THE AICME OF *EABHADH*
(EA, OI, UI, IO, AI)

Name	Roman letter	Tree Color
Eabhadh	EA	Aspen-green
Oir	OI	Spindle-white
Uinllean	UI	Honeysuckle-tawny
Ifin	IO	Gooseberry-white
Amancholl	AI	Pine (Rainbow)

Classification of
Celtic Tree Types

The *Book of Ballymote* lists the following:

Royal or Chieftain Trees (8): Elm, Oak, Hazel, Vine, Ivy, Blackthorn, Broom, Spindle.

Kiln or Peasant Trees (8): Birch, Rowan, Willow, Ash, Whitethorn, Fig, Apple, Cork.

Spiral or Green Trees (8): names not given.

Traditional Irish Brehon Law (IV, 147) lists seven Chieftain Trees, seven Peasant Trees, seven Shrub Trees, and eight Bushes:

Chieftain Trees: *Dair* (Oak), *Coll* (Hazel), *Cuileann* (Holly), *Ibur* (Yew), *Iundius* (Ash), *Ochtach* (Fir), *Aball* (Apple).

Peasant Trees: *Fernn* (Alder), *Sail* (Willow), *Scaith* (Whitethorn), *Caerthann* (Rowan), *Beithe* (Birch), *Learn* (Elm), *Idha* (Ivy).

Shrub Trees: *Draidean* (Blackthorn), *Trom* (Elder), *Fincoll* (White Hazel), *Crithach* (Aspen), *Caithne* (Strawberry Tree), *Feorus* (uncertain), *Crann-Fir* (uncertain).

Bushes: *Raith* (Fern), *Rait* (uncertain), *Aiteand* (Gorse), *Dris* (Dog Rose), *Freach* (Heather), *Eideand* (uncertain), *Gilcoch* (Broom), *Spin* (Spindle). (Joyce 1903, II:286–87)

Appendix 3

The Bardic Hierarchy

In Welsh tradition, the chief Bard, "who has won a competition for a chair," is called *pencerdd*. In Irish society, this rank was paralleled by the *ollam* (chief *fili*). Next in precedence below the pencerdd comes the *bardd teulu*, a court Bard whose symbol of office was a harp given to him by his lord, with which he must never part. He sang to the warriors before a raid and sang "The Monarchy of Britain" to them before a battle. The lower-ranking Bards are the *cerddorion* (minstrels) and, below them, the *croesaniaid* (buffoons, fools, and ribald rhymers). The use of the *ffon wen* (the "white stick," a freshly peeled hazel stick sent anonymously to a rejected lover) may be a continuation of the practices of the croesaniaid.

This lowest rank appears to be equivalent to the Irish *crossáin* (sg. *crosán*), who went around in bands. There is an ancient Irish account of nine such "black and hairy" figures who chanted all night on the fresh grave of a dead king. They were expelled by Christian priests at dawn. Linked to these were the satirists (who have their parallel in the contemporary *Schandtle* of the Swabian-Allemannic *Fastnacht*). The ancient laws of Ireland called them the "sons of death and bad men," and ranked them among "fools, jesters, buffoons, outlaws, heathens, harlots—who hold demon banquets" (Rees and Rees 1967, 128).

Glossary of Terms

Key to Abbreviations:

Corn.	Cornish	OIr.	Old Irish
Eng.	English	ON	Old Norse
Ger.	German	PCelt.	Proto-Celtic
Gk	Greek	S	Scots
I	Irish	W	Welsh
Lat.	Latin		

abcedilros: in Bardo-Druidic lore, the earliest British alphabet of ten letters (W).

Abred: in Bardo-Druidic lore, the middle world (W).

aibítir: alphabet (I).

aicme: group of five Oghams (I).

aiteann: Furze (I).

Alba: the old Irish name for Scotland (I).

Annwn (Annwvyn): in Bardo-Druidic lore, the lower world; also known as "the loveless place," "the land invisible," and the Abyss (W).

An Ogham Craobh: "the (tree-)branch Ogham," the basic form of Ogham (I).

ánradh: chief poet of second order (I).

ardrí: the high king of Ireland (I).

arris: the edge or corner of a dressed stone.

awen: spirit, the power of inspiration; the Bardic and Druidic threefold symbol of the divine spark (W).

awenyddion (sg. *awenydd*): inspired poets or oracles (W).

bannock: a ceremonial biscuit or cake (S).

Bard: a traditional poet, historian, and genealogist of Celtic society, often part of a royal or lordly household, charged with composing songs of commemoration or praise for individuals; in nineteenth-century Bardo-Druidic lore, conflated with the functions of a Druid and given a semi-religious function.

Bardd teulu: court Bard, serving a lord (W).

Beltane: the Celtic May festival, starting at sunset on April 30; also referred to as Cétshamain ("the first of summer"). *Cormac's Glossary* states: "BELLTAINE 'May-Day' i.e. *bil-tene*, lucky fire" (O'Donovan 1868, 19); and the *Etymological Dictionary of the Scottish Language*: "Beltane, Beltein. The name of a sort of festival observed on the first of May, O.S. [Old Style]; hence used to denote the term of Whitsunday" (Jamieson 1808, 161).

Beith: "Birch," the first letter of the Ogham alphabet (I).

Beth–Luis–Nion (B, L, N): name for the Ogham alphabet based on a variant (and allegedly more ancient) ordering of the first three letters (I).

bodhrán: Irish goatskin drum, traditionally played in a Wren Boys procession on St. Stephen's Day or Boxing Day (December 26).

broom-cow: ceremonial besom of heather (S).

burin: tool for carving Oghams (I).

Caledonia: the old name for the territory that became Scotland after the Scots (from Ireland) invaded and conquered it (Lat.).

caorthann: Rowan (Mountain Ash) tree (I).

celyn: Holly (W).

cerddorion (sg. *cerddor*): medieval minstrels (W).

Ceugant: in Bardo-Druidic lore, the transcendent upper realm of the ineffable source (W).

cláirseach: Irish harp (I).

codi'r fedwen: "raising the birch," the Welsh ceremony of raising the Maypole (W).

coelbren: "lots" or, in Bardo-Druidic lore, letters carved into wood (W).

coelvain: in Bardo-Druidic lore, letters carved into stone (especially slate) (W).

coll: Hazel tree (I).

collen: Hazel tree (W).

comraich: sacred enclosure around a holy place (e.g., a church) (S).

crannog: artificial island on piles (such as a lake village) (I).

craobh: a line or whole series of Ogham characters; a "branch, bough" (I).

criafol: Rowan (W).

croesaniaid (sg. *croesan*): buffoons, fools, jesters, ribald rhymers (W).

crosáin (sg. *crosán*): buffoons, fools, jesters, satirists, ribald rhymers (I).

cuileann: Holly tree (I).

Cymry: the Welsh people (W).

cyntevin: the beginning of Summer (W).

cyrven: in Bardo-Druidic lore, a letter burnt on wood by pyrography (W).

cwywdd: Welsh poem in traditional meter (W).

dair: Oak tree (I).

Daronwy: "The Thunderer," byname of God from a poem of the same name in *The Book of Taliesin* (W).

dawns y fedwen: the Maypole dance (lit. "dance of the Birch") (W).

Derwen: Oak tree (W).

draighean: Blackthorn (I).

draoi: wizard (I).

dris: Bramble (I). *See* sméar dhubh.

druí: Druid (OIr.).

Druid: Pagan Celtic priest (ultimately from PCelt. *druwits*, "tree-knower"); cf. *druí* (OIr.), *draoidh* (S).

druim: the "ridge" or "line" on which Ogham characters are written (I).

Dumnonia: the old Celtic country covering the present counties of Devon and Cornwall in southwestern England (from the Cornish tribal name of the Dumnonii).

ebill (pl. *ebillion*): in Bardo-Druidic lore, a board or rod with letters (W).

eiddew: Ivy (W).

eidhneán: Ivy (I).

Fastnacht (*Fasnacht*, *Fasnet*, etc.): the period of "carnival" and "misrule" leading up to Shrove Tuesday (Ger.).

feá: Beech tree (I).

fedwen haf: the Summer Birch (midsummer pole) (W)

feisefin: Ogham wheel, otherwise "Fionn's Wheel," "Fionn's Window," or "Fionn's Shield" (I).

ffon wen: the "white stick," a Hazel rod used for insults (W).

fidh or *fid* (pl. *feadha* or *feda*): a "letter" in Ogham; a "tree" (I).

fili (pl. *filidh* or **filid**): ancient Irish poet (OIr.).

fleasc filidh: a Bardic wand (I).

flesc (pl. *flesca*): a cut or line of an Ogham character; a "twig" (I).

forfeada: "overtrees," the fifth *aicme* of the Oghams (I). *See* aicme.

fraoch: Heather (I).

fuinseog: Ash tree (I).

Gaeilge: the indigenous Celtic language of Ireland (I). *See also* Gael and Gaelic.

Gael: an early medieval name for ethnic Irish people (including Scots) (I).

Gaelic: the Celtic language of Scotland (Eng.).

gall: an early medieval name for non-Irish (foreigners) (I).

gangen haf: the Summer Branch (W).

geis (pl. *geasa*): a magical prohibition (taboo) (I).

Geranos: the Crane-Dance of the labyrinth (from Gk. γέρανος).

ghuaim: a term for wisdom found in the *Book of Ballymote* (I).

giolcach: Reed (I).

giúis: Fir or Pine tree (I).

gwyddoniaid (sg. *gwyddon*): the men of letters, people endowed with reason and learning, i.e., Druids, Ovates, or Bards (W).

Gwynvyd: in Bardo-Druidic lore, the spiritual upper world (lit. the "White Land") (W).

holmganga: lit. "going on an island"; ritual combat in a specially delimited area (ON).

höslur: "hazles" or hazel-poles used to delimit the ritual enclosure known as the *völlr haslaðr*, "enhazeled field," a sacred enclosure for ritual combat (ON).

iúr: Yew tree (I).

kenning: a traditional type of poetic allusion, such as "horse of the sea" for ship (Eng.).

kvistrúnar: "twig-runes," a system of runic encryption resembling Ogham (ON).

limewood: wood of the Linden tree (*Tilia platyphyllos*) (Eng.).

list: a fenced area used in tournaments and medieval ritual combat.

litir (pl. *litreacha*): a letter in the Gaelic *aibítir* (I). *See* aibítir.

llan: sacred enclosure around a holy place (e.g., a church) (W). *See also* comraich.

llythrau: in Bardo-Druidic lore, Coelbren letters cut on wood.

Lunantishee: guardian sprite of the Blackthorn (*straif*) (I).

May Tree: Whitethorn (*Crataegus monogyna*) (Eng.).

May Tree: Maypole (Eng.).

mete-wand: measuring-stick (in Irish context, a rod for measuring the dead) (Eng.).

Muc Ogham: color ogham (OIr.).

Muime: mythological monster from Scandinavia that destroyed the Wood of Caledon in Scotland (S).

Narrenbaum: "fools' tree," the pole erected at *Fastnacht* (Shrovetide) in south Germany (Ger.).

Narrenzunft: fools' guild (Ger.).

nemeton: sanctuary, often a sacred grove of trees (from PCelt. *nemetom*).

nimidas: term for "ceremonies of the woodland" in a Carolingian index prohibiting pagan practices (ultimately from PCelt. *nemetom*).

nodaighe: "certain abbreviations" in medieval Irish cryptography (I).

Ogham (Ogam, Ogum): ancient Celtic alphabet used in Ireland and the British Isles; a "tree alphabet" according to certain interpretations dating back to the medieval period (I).

Oíche Shamhna: Hallowe'en/All Saints' Day (I). *See* Samhain.

ollam: (lit. "supreme" or "most transcendent") master-poet (chief poet of the first order) of Ireland. A title once used for the chief of every hierarchy (I).

omphalos: a central place of assembly and oracles (from Gk. ὀμφᾰλός, "navel of the world").

onnen: Ash tree (W).

ovate: a diviner or ritual specialist (from Gk. οὐᾰτεις, ultimately from PCelt. *watis*); according to modern Druidic lore, ascribed a green robe. *See also* vates.

peithenyn: in Bardo-Druidic lore, a wooden frame holding wooden bars with writing (W).

peithynvain: in Bardo-Druidic lore, the "stones of elucidation": Welsh Bardic stone tablets (W).

pencerdd: chief Bard "who has won a competition for a chair" (W).

pill: splinter (W).

pillwydd: in Bardo-Druidic lore, a wooden bar with letters (W).

pisky: a Cornish sprite; cf. English "pixie" (Corn.).

plagawd: in Bardo-Druidic lore, an ancient form of paper made from a sedge or papyrus and believed to be imported to Britain from India by the Romans (W).

pren: wood (Middle Welsh *prenn*) (W).

pylgeint: dawn (W).

rhabdomancy: divining for water or metal using a rod (Eng.).

rhabdomant: a practitioner of rhabdomancy (Eng.).

rune: character in the Germanic/Norse magical alphabet (Ger., Eng.).

sailech: Willow tree (I).

Samhain: [pronounced SOW-ain] modern name for the old Celtic festival that included Samhnag (S), Lá Samhna (I), and Oíche Shamhna (I), Christianized as Holymas /All Saints' Day; the beginning of the old Celtic year, commencing at sunset on October 31 (I). *See* Oíche Shamhna.

sceach: Hawthorn (Whitethorn) (I).

Scotia: ancient name for Ireland (I).

Shrovetide: the days leading up to Shrove Tuesday (Eng.).

sméar dhubh: Blackberry, brambleberry (I). *See* dris.

spíonán: Gooseberry (I).

Tabhall lorga: "tablet staves," symbol of office of Bards (I).

Taibhli filidh: "tablets of the poets" (I).

Tamlorga filidh: "staves of the poets" (I).

temenos: sacred enclosure around a temple (Gk.).

trom: Elder tree (I).

vates: Pagan Celtic diviner (Lat.).

vébönd: sacred enclosure with Hazel posts linked by rope (ON).

Whitethorn: Hawthorn or May Tree (*Crataegus monogyna*; Ogham *Huath*) (Eng.).

Bibliography and Resources
for Further Study

A. E. [= "Æ," George William Russell]. 1918. *A Candle of Vision*. London: Macmillan.

Abbott, Mike. 1989. *Green Woodwork: Working with Wood the Natural Way*. London: Guild of Master Craftsmen.

Anderson, Joseph. 1868. *Scotland in Pagan Times*. Edinburgh: Douglas.

[Anon. = His Majesty's Commissioners]. 1946. *The Royal Commission on the Ancient Monuments of Scotland Twelfth Report with an Inventory of the Ancient Monuments of Orkney and Shetland. Volume III: Inventory of Shetland*. Edinburgh: H.M.S.O.

Anwyl, Edward. 1906. *Celtic Religion*. London: Constable.

———. 1907. "Ancient Celtic Goddesses." *The Celtic Review* 3: 26–51.

Arntz, Helmut. 1935. "Das Ogom." *Beiträge zur Geschichte der deutschen Sprache und Literatur* 59: 321–413.

Atkinson, George Mouncey. 1874. "Some Account of Ancient Irish Treatises on Ogham Writing, Illustrated by Tracings from the Original MSS." *Journal of the Royal Historical and Archaeological Association of Ireland*. Fourth Series, vol. 3, no. 19 (Jul.): 202–236.

Atkinson, Robert, ed. 1880. *The Book of Leinster, sometime called the Book of Glendalough: a collection of pieces (prose and verse) in the Irish language; compiled in part about the middle of the twelfth century*. Dublin: Royal Irish Academy.

Auld, William Muir. 1931. *Christmas*. London: Macmillan.

Bamford, Christopher, and William Price Marsh. 1986. *Celtic Christianity*. Edinburgh: Floris.

Baring, Anne, and Jules Cashford. 1993. *The Myth of the Goddess.* London: Book Club Associates.

Baring-Gould, Sabine. 1909. *A Book of Devon.* London: Methuen.

Baring-Gould, Sabine, and John Fisher. 1913. *The Lives of the British Saints.* 4 vols. London: Honourable Society of Cymmrodorion.

Barrett, Francis. 1801. *The Magus, or Celestial Intelligencer; Being a Complete System of Occult Philosophy.* London: Lackington, Allen, and Co.

Bartsch, Albert. 1993. *Holz Masken, Fastnachts- und Maskenbrauchtum in der Schweiz, in Süddeutschland und Osterreich.* Aarau: AT Verlag.

Basford, Kathleen. 1978. *The Green Man.* Ipswich: Brewer.

Bernard, J. H., and R. Atkinson. 1898. *The Irish "Liber hymnorum": Edited from the mss., with Translations, Notes and Glossary.* 2 vols. London: Henry Bradshaw Society.

Berners, Juliana, ed. 1901. *The Boke of Saint Albans.* London: Stock.

Binchy, D. A. 1958. "The Fair of Tailtu and the Feast of Tara." *Eriu* 18: 113–36.

Black, Joseph, et al., eds. 2015. *The Broadview Anthology of British Literature.* 6 vols. Peterborough, Ont.: Broadview.

Blake, Lois. 1972. *Traditional Dance and Customs in Wales.* Llangollen: Gwynn.

Bonwick, James. 1894. *Irish Druids and Old Irish Religions.* London: Sampson, Low, Marston and Co.

Bossert, Helmuth T. 1953. *Folk Art of Europe.* London: Praeger.

Botticher, Carl. 1856. *Der Baumkultus der Hellenen.* Berlin: Zwemmer.

Bowen, Dewi. 1992. *Ancient Siluria.* Llanerch: Felinfach.

Bowen, E. G. 1956. *The Settlements of the Celtic Saints in Wales.* Cardiff: University of Wales Press.

Breathnach, Breandán. 1986. *Folk Music and Dances of Ireland.* Dublin: Mercier.

Brekilien, Yann. 1981. *La mythologie celtique.* Paris: Editions Jean Picollec.

Brewer, E. Cobham. 1900. *Dictionary of Phrase and Fable.* Revised and expanded edition. London: Cassell.

Broadwood, Lucy E., and J. A. Fuller Maitland. 1893. *English County Songs.* London: Leadenhall.

Bromwich, Rachel. 1979. *Trioedd Ynys Prydein: The Welsh Triads.* Cardiff: University of Wales Press.

Brosse, Jacques. 1989. *Mythologie des arbres.* Paris: Pion.

Brown, Theo. 1979. *The Fate of the Dead: Folk Eschatology in the West Country after the Reformation.* Cambridge: Brewer.

Brunaux, Jean-Louis. 1988. *The Celtic Gauls: Gods, Rites and Sanctuaries.* London: Seaby.

Bryce, Derek. 1989. *Symbolism of the Celtic Cross.* Llandyssul: Gomer.

Bucknell, Peter A. 1979. *Entertainment and Ritual 600–1600.* London: Stainer and Bell.

Byrne, Patrick F. 1967. *Witchcraft in Ireland.* Cork: Mercier.

Calder, George, ed. and trans. 1917. *Auraicept na n-Éces—The Scholars' Primer, being the texts of the Ogham tract from the Book of Ballymote and the Yellow Book of Lecan, and the text of the Trefhocul from the Book of Leinster.* Edinburgh: Grant.

Campbell, John Gregorson. 1900. *Superstitions of the Highlands and Islands of Scotland.* Glasgow: MacLehouse and Sons.

Carmichael, Alexander. 1940. *Carmina Gadelica: Hymns and Incantations.* Edinburgh: Oliver and Boyd.

Cawte, E. C. 1978. *Ritual Animal Disguise.* Cambridge: Brewer.

Chadwick, N. K. 1942. *Poetry and Prophecy.* Cambridge: Cambridge University Press.

Christian, Roy. 1974. *Old English Customs.* Newton Abbot: David and Charles.

Clarus, Ingeborg. 1991. *Keltische Mythen: Der Mensch und seine Anderswelt.* Olten: Walter.

Close-Brooks, J., and R. B. K. Stevenson. 1982. *Dark Age Sculpture: A Selection from Collections of the National Museum of Antiquities of Scotland.* Edinburgh: Royal Commission on Historic Monuments.

Condren, Mary. 1989. *The Serpent and the Goddess: Women, Religion and Power in Celtic Ireland,* San Francisco: Harper and Row.

Constantine, Mary-Anne. 2007. *The Truth against the World: Iolo Morganwg and Romantic Forgery.* Cardiff: Unversity of Wales Press.

Cook, Arthur Bernard. 1906. "The European Sky-God, IV: The Celts." *Folklore* 17.1: 27–71.

Cooper, Emmanuel. 1994. *People's Art.* Edinburgh and London: Mainstream.

Corkery, Daniel. 1925. *The Hidden Ireland: A Study of Gaelic Munster in the Eighteenth Century.* Dublin: Gill and Son.

Cross, Teresa. 2020. *Secrets of the Druids: From Indo-European Origins to Modern Practices.* Rochester, VT: Inner Traditions.

Cross, Tom Peete, and Clark Harris Slover. 1936. *Ancient Irish Tales.* New York: Holt.

Crossing, William. 1902. *The Ancient Stone Crosses of Dartmoor and Its Borderland*. Exeter: Commin.

Cubbon, A. M. 1971. *The Art of Manx Crosses*. Douglas: Manx Museum and National Trust.

Culpeper, Nicholas. 1832. *The Complete Herbal*. Expanded edition. London: Smith.

Cunnack, Edward M. 1968. *The Helston Furry Dance*. Helston: Flora Day Association and the Stewards of the Helston Furry Dance.

Daniell, S. 1970. *Old Cornwall: Life in the County About a Century Ago*. Truro: Tor Mark.

Dannheimer, Hermann, and Rupert Gebhard. 1993. *Das keltische Jahrtausend*. Mainz: Philipp Von Zabern.

Darkstar, Erynn. 1990a. "Ogham, Tree-Lore and The Celtic Tree Oracle: Searching for Roots, Pt. 1." *Manteia* 3: 29–31.

———. 1990b. "Ogham, Tree-Lore and The Celtic Tree Oracle: Searching for Roots, Pt. 2." *Manteia* 4: 32–35.

———. 1991. "Ogham, Tree-Lore and The Celtic Tree Oracle: Searching for Roots, Pt. 3." *Manteia* 6: 22–25.

———. 1992. "Ogham, Tree-Lore and The Celtic Tree Oracle: Searching for Roots, Pt. 3 (cont.)." *Manteia* 7: 22–24.

Davidson, Hilda Ellis. 1988. *Myths and Symbols in Pagan Europe: Early Scandinavian and Celtic Religions*. Manchester: Manchester University Press.

Davies, Morgan T. 1995. "*Aed I'r coed i doni cof*: Dafydd ap Gwilym and the Metaphorics of Carpentry." *Cambrian Medieval Celtic Studies* 30 (Winter): 67–85.

Davies, Jonathan Ceredig. 1911. *Folk-lore of West and Mid-Wales*. Aberystwyth: University of Wales Press.

Davies, Wendy. 1982. *Wales in the Early Middle Ages*. Leicester: Leicester University Press.

Deeney, Daniel. 1901. *Peasant Lore from Gaelic Ireland*. London: Nutt.

Denyer, Susan. 1991. *Traditional Buildings and Life in the Lake District*. London: Gollancz/Crawley.

De Paor, Maire, and Liam de Paor. 1958. *Early Christian Ireland*. London: Thames and Hudson.

De Vries, Jan. 1961. *Keltische Religion*. Stuttgart: Kohlhammer.

Dillon, Mary, ed. 2014. *Aibítir: The Irish Alphabet in Botanical Art*. Dublin: The Society of Botanical Artists.

Dillon, Myles. 1948. *Early Irish Literature*. Chicago: University of Chicago Press.

———. ed. and trans. 1951–1952. "The Taboos of the Kings of Ireland." *Proceedings of the Royal Irish Academy* 54: 1–6, 8–25, 27–36.

Dillon, Myles, and Nora K. Chadwick. 1973. *The Celtic Realms*. London: Cardinal.

Dinneen, Patrick S. 1927. *Foclóir Gaedhilge agus Béarla—An Irish-English Dictionary*. Dublin: Irish Texts Society.

Dontenville, Henri. 1948. *La mythologie française*. Paris: Payot.

Drake-Camell, F. J. 1938. *Old English Customs and Ceremonies*. London: Batsford.

Dumézil, Georges. 1952. *Les dieux des indo-européens*. Paris: PUF.

Ellis, Peter Berresford. 1989. *Dictionary of Irish Mythology*. London: Constable.

———. 1992. *Dictionary of Celtic Mythology*. London: Constable.

Ellis, T. P. 1926. *Welsh Tribal Law and Custom*. Oxford: Clarendon.

Evans, E. Estyn. 1957. *Irish Folk Ways*. London: Routledge and Kegan Paul.

Evans, John Gwenogvryn, ed. 1906. *The Black Book of Carmarthen*. Pwllheli: N.p.

———. ed. 1910. *The Text of the Book of Taliesin*. Llanbedrog: N.p.

———. ed. 1911. *The Poetry from the Red Book of Hergest*. Llanbedrog: N.p.

Evans-Wentz, W. Y. 1911. *The Fairy Faith in Celtic Countries*. Oxford: Oxford University Press.

Favyn, A. 1623. *A Theater of Honour and Knight-Hood*. London: Jaggard.

Ferguson, Samuel. 1887. *Ogham Inscriptions in Ireland, Wales, and Scotland*. Edinburgh: Douglas.

Fischer-Rizzi, Susanne. 1980. *Blätter von Bäumen, Legenden, Mythen, Heilanwendung und Betrachtung von einheimischen Baumen*. Haldenwang: Irisiana.

Fitzpatrick, Jim. 1985. *Erinsaga*. Dublin: De Danaan.

Frampton, George. 1992. *Grovely! Grovely! and all Grovely! The History of Oak Apple Day in Great Wishford*. York: Quacks.

Gantz, Jeffrey. 1976. *The Mabinogion*. Harmondsworth: Penguin.

———. 1981. *Early Irish Myths and Sagas*. London: Penguin.

Gerald of Wales. 1978. *The Journey Through Wales / The Description of Wales*. Translated by Lewis Thorpe. London: Penguin.

Gerard, John. 1969. *Leaves from Gerard's Herball*. Edited by Marcus Woodward. New York: Dover.

Gercke, Hans, ed. 1985. *Der Baum in Mythologie, Kunstgeschichte und Gegenwartskunst*. Heidelberg: Braus.

Gerschel, L. 1959. "Origine et premier usage des caractères Ogamiques." *Ogam* 9: 151–73.

Graham, Frank. 1965. *Old Inns and Taverns of Yorkshire (North Riding).* Newcastle-upon-Tyne: Graham.

Graves, Charles. 1876. "The Ogham Alphabet." *Hermathena* 2: 443–72.

Graves, Robert. 1966. *The White Goddess.* Amended and enlarged edition. New York: Farrar, Straus and Giroux.

Green, Miranda. 1986. *The Gods of the Celts.* Gloucester: Sutton.

———. 1989. *Symbol and Image in Celtic Religious Art.* London: Routledge.

Greer, John Michael. 2017. *The Coelbren Alphabet: The Forgotten Oracle of the Welsh Bards.* Woodbury, MN: Llewellyn. [Retitled, revised, and expanded edition: *Coelbren: Traditions, Divination Lore, and Magic of the Welsh Bardic Alphabet.* N.p.: Aeon, 2023.]

Gregory, Lady. 1911. *Cuchulain of Muirthemne.* London: Murray.

Grinsell, L. V. 1976. *Folklore of Prehistoric Sites in Britain.* Newton Abbot: David and Charles.

Guénon, René. 1927. *Le Roi du Monde.* Paris: Bosse.

Guyonvarc'h, Christian-J. 1980. *Textes mythologiques irlandais.* Rennes: Ogam-Celticum.

Gwynn, Edward J., ed. and trans. 1903–1935. *The Metrical Dindschenchas.* 5 vols. Dublin: Hodges, Figgis, and Co.

Hardy, Philip Dixon. 1840. *The Holy Wells of Ireland.* Dublin: Hardy and Walder.

Harte, Frank, ed. 1993. *Songs of Dublin.* Cork: Ossian.

Harte, Jeremy. 1996. "Herne the Hunter—A Case of Mistaken Identity?" *At The Edge* 3: 27–33.

Hartmann, Hans. 1952. *Der Totenkult in Irland: Ein Beitrag zur Religion der Indogermanen.* Heidelberg: Winter.

Hatt, Jean-Jacques. 1970. *Celts and Gallo-Romans.* London: Barrie and Jenkins.

Helm, Alex. 1981. *The Mummers' Play.* Ipswich: Brewer.

Henderson, G. 1911. *Survivals in Belief among the Celts.* Glasgow: MacLehose and Sons.

Herbert, Henri. 1925. "Le Mythe d'Epona." In *Mélanges linguistiques offerts à M. J. Vendreyes par ses amis,* edited by Louis Renou. Paris: Champion.

Herrick, Robert. 1902. *The Poems of Robert Herrick.* London: Richards.

Hesse, Hermann. 1984. *Bäume: Betrachtungen und Gedichte.* Frankfurt am Main: Insel.

Hetmann, Frederik, ed. 1988. *Baum und Zauber*. Munich: Goldmann.

———. 1984. *Irischer Zaubergarten: Märchen, Sagen und Geschichten von der grünen Insel*. Frankfurt: Fischer.

Hogan, Eileen. 1978. *Ogham: Each Letter of the Alphabet is Presented with a Colour and a Bird*. London: Burnt Wood.

Howell, James. 1644. *Dodona's Grove, Or The Vocall Forrest*. London: N.p.

Hughes, A. Lloyd. 1979. "The Welsh Folk Museum Manuscripts." *Folklife* 17: 68–70.

Hull, Eleanor. 1911. *Cuchulain: The Hound of Ulster*. London: Harrap.

———. 1928. *Folklore of the British Isles*. London: Methuen.

Hutton, Ronald. 1994. *The Rise and Fall of Merrie England*. Oxford: Oxford University Press.

———. 1996. *The Stations of the Sun: A History of the Ritual Year in Britain*. Oxford: Oxford University Press.

———. 2009. *Blood and Mistletoe: The History of the Druids in Britain*. New Haven: Yale University Press.

Jackson, Kenneth H. A. 1951. *A Celtic Miscellany*. London: Routledge and Kegan Paul.

———. 1953. *Language and History in Early Britain: A Chronological Survey of the Brittonic Languages 1st to 12th c. A.D*. Edinburgh: Edinburgh University Press.

———. 1950. "Notes on the Ogham Inscriptions of Southern Britain." In *Early Cultures of North West Europe*, edited by Cyril Fox and Bruce Dickins. London.

Jackson, Nigel. 1995a. *Call of the Horned Piper*. Chieveley: Capall Bann.

Jackson, Nigel. 1995b. *Masks of Misrule—The Horned God and His Cult in Europe*. Chieveley: Capall Bann.

Jackson, Nigel, and Nigel Pennick. *The New Celtic Oracle*. Chieveley: Capall Bann, 1997.

Jacobsthal, Paul. 1944. *Early Celtic Art*. Oxford: Clarendon.

James, David, ed. 1999. *Celtic Arts and Crafts Planetary Directory 1999*. Portesham: Celtic Connections.

James, David, and Stuart Booth, eds. 1999. *Visions in Celtic Art: The Modern Tradition*, London: Blandford.

James, E. O. 1961. *Seasonal Feasts and Festivals*. London: Thames and Hudson.

Jamieson, John. 1818. *Etymological Dictionary of the Scottish Language*. Abridged edition. Edinburgh: Constable and Co., and Jameson.

Jensen, K. Frank. 1985. *The Prophetic Cards—A Catalog of Cards for Fortune-telling*. Roskilde: Ouroboros.

———. 1990. *The Prophetic Cards II: 110 More Fortune-telling Decks*. Roskilde: Ouroboros.

Joliffe, Norah. 1941. "Dea Brigantia." *Archaeological Journal* 98: 36–61.

Jones, David. 1959. *Epoch and Artist*. London: Faber.

Jones, Francis. 1954. *The Holy Wells of Wales*. Cardiff: University of Wales Press.

Jones, Gwyn, and Thomas Jones, trans. 1948. *The Mabinogion*. London: Dent.

Jones, Kelvin I., ed. 1997. *Strange Cornish Customs*. Penzance: Oakmagic.

Jones, Owen, Edward Williams, and William Owen Pughe, eds. 1870. *The Myrvyrian Archaiology of Wales*. Denbigh: Gee.

Jones, Prudence, and Nigel Pennick. 1995. *A History of Pagan Europe*. London: Routledge.

Joseph, Lionel S., and Brian Drayton. 2020–2021. "Trees and Tradition in Early Ireland." *Studia Celtica Fennica* 17: 54–73.

Joyce, P. W. 1903. *A Social History of Ancient Ireland*. 2 vols. London: Longmans, Green, and Co.

Judge, Roy. 1977. *The Jack in the Green: A May Day Custom*. Cambridge: Brewer.

Jung, Carl Gustav. 1971. *The Archetypes and the Collective Unconscious*. London: Routledge and Kegan Paul.

———. 1964. *Man and His Symbols*. London: Aldus.

Kaul, Flemming, Ivan Marazov, Jan Best, and Nanny De Vries. 1991. *Thracian Tales on the Gundestrup Cauldron*. Amsterdam: Najade.

Keiller, Alexander. 1965. *Windmill Hill and Avebury Excavations, 1925–1939*. Oxford: Oxford University Press.

Kennedy, Patrick. 1891. *Legendary Fictions of the Irish Celts*. London: Macmillan.

Kennedy, Peter, ed. 1984. *Folksongs of Britain and Ireland*. London: Oak.

Keverne, Richard. 1955. *Tales of Old Inns*. London: Collins.

King, John. 1994. *The Celtic Druids' Year*. London: Blandford.

Kinsella, Thomas, trans. 1985. *The Táin*. Philadelphia: University of Philadelphia Press.

Kirke, John. 1638. *The Seven Champions of Christendome*. London.

Knott, Eleanor, ed. 1936. *Togail Bruidne Da Derga*. Dublin: *Dublin* Institute for Advanced Studies.

Lainé-Kerjean, C. 1943. "Le Calendrier Celtique." *Zeitschrift für celtische Philologie* 23: 249–84.

Laing, Lloyd. 1975. *The Archaeology of Late Celtic Britain and Ireland c. 400–1200 AD*. London: Methuen.

Lambert, Margaret, and Enid Marx. 1989. *English Popular Art*. London: Merlin.

Larwood, Jacob, and John Camden Hotten. 1951 [1866]. *English Inn Signs*. London: Chatto and Windus.

Leather, Ella Mary. 1912. *The Folk-lore of Herefordshire*. Hereford and London: Jakeman and Carver / Sidgwick and Jackson.

Le Braz, Anatole. 1893. *La Légende de la Mort en Basse-Bretagne*. Paris: Champion.

———. 1906. *The Land of Pardons*. Translated by Frances M. Gostling. London: Methuen.

Ledwich, Edward. 1804. *The Antiquities of Ireland*. Second expanded edition. Dublin: Jones.

Le Goff, Jacques. 1988. *The Medieval Imagination*. Chicago: University of Chicago Press.

Lehmacher, G. 1949–1950. "The Ancient Celtic Year." *Journal of Celtic Studies* 1: 144–47.

Lengyel, Lancelot. 1969. *Le Secret des Celtes*. Paris: Morel.

Leslie, Shane. 1932. *Saint Patrick's Purgatory: A Record from History and Literature*. London: Burns, Oates and Washbourne.

Lightfoot, John. 1777. *Flora Scotica: or, a Systematic Arrangement in the Linnaean Method, of the Native Plants of Scotland and the Hebrides*. 2 vols. London.

Little, George A. 1957. *Dublin Before the Vikings*. Dublin: Gill and Son.

Lorenzoni, Piero. 1984. *English Eroticism*. Ware: Omega.

Lucan [Marcus Annaeus Lucanus]. 1928. *The Civil War: Books I–X (Pharsalia)*. Translated by J. D. Duff. London: Heinemann.

Luzel, F. M. 1985. *Celtic Folk Tales from Armorica*. Translated by Derek Bryce. Lampeter: Llanerch.

Macalister, R. A. S. 1897–1907. *Studies in Irish Epigraphy*. 3 vols. London: Nutt.

———. 1928. *The Archeology of Ireland*. London: Methuen.

———. 1937. *The Secret Languages of Ireland*. Cambridge: Cambridge University Press.

———, ed. and trans. 1938–1956. *Lebor gabála Érenn: The Book of the Taking of Ireland*. 4 vols. Dublin Irish Texts Society.

———. 1945. *Corpus Inscriptionum Insularum Celticarum*. Dublin: Irish Texts Society.

MacCana, Proinsias. 1970. *Celtic Mythology.* London: Hamlyn.

MacCulloch, John Arnott. 1991. *The Religion of the Ancient Celts.* London: Constable.

Macleod, Fiona. 1902. "Sea Magic and Running Water." *The Contemporary Review* 82: 573–34.

MacManus, Dermot. 1959. *The Middle Kingdom.* Gerrard's Cross: Smythe.

MacNeill, Eoin. [1934]. *Early Irish Laws and Institutions.* Dublin: Burns, Oates and Washbourne.

MacNeill, M. 1962. *The Festival of Lughnasa.* Oxford: Oxford University Press.

Macqueen, J. 1954. "Maponus in Medieval Tradition." *Transactions of the Dumfries and Galloway Natural History and Antiquarian Society* 31: 43–57.

Maier, Bernhard. 1994. *Dictionary of Celtic Religion and Culture.* Translated by Cyril Edwards. Woodbridge: Boydell.

Male, Emil. 1950. *Le fin du paganisme en Gaule.* Paris: Flammarion.

Matthews, John. 1991. *Taliesin.* London: Aquarian.

Matthews, John, and R. J. Stewart. 1987. *Warriors of Arthur.* London: Blandford.

McManus, Damian. 1991. *A Guide to Ogam.* Maynooth: An Sagart.

———. 1988. "Irish Letter-Names and their Kennings." *Ériu* 39: 127–68.

McNeill, F. Marian. 1989. *The Silver Bough.* Edinburgh: Canongate.

Meme, John. 1974. *A Handbook of Celtic Ornament.* Dublin: Mercier.

Meroney, Howard. 1949. "Early Irish Letter-Names." *Speculum* 24.1: 19–43.

Meyer, Kuno, trans. 1901. "The Expulsion of the Dessi." *Y Cymmrodor* 14: 101–135.

———, ed. and trans. 1906. *The Triads of Ireland.* Dublin: Hodges, Figgis, and Co.

Meyrick, Samuel Rush. 1808. *The History and Antiquities of the County of Cardiganshire.* London: Longman, Hurst, Rees, and Orme.

Milton, Roger. 1972. *The English Ceremonial Book: A History of Robes, Insignia and Ceremonies still in use in England.* Newton Abbot: David and Charles.

Monson-Fitzjohn, G. J. 1926. *Quaint Signs of Olde Inns.* London: Herbert Jenkins.

Murphy, Gerard. 1956. *Early Irish Lyrics, 8th–12th century.* Oxford: Clarendon.

Murray, Colin. 1977. *Ogham Divination Card Game.* Golden Section Order, London.

———. 1979a. "Ogham Chart." *Newsletter of the Golden Section Order, The Bardic Chair of Caer Llyndain*, August issue.

———. 1979b. "The Trees of the Forest." *Newsletter of the Golden Section Order, The Bardic Chair of Caer Llyndain*, August issue.

Murray, Liz, and Colin Murray. 1988. *The Celtic Tree Oracle*. Artwork by Vanessa Card. London: Rider.

Naddair, Kaledon. 1984. *Koelbren Cards* I. Artwork by Edwin O'Donnelly, et al. Edinburgh: Inner Keltia.

———. 1986. *Koelbren Cards* II. Artwork by Lorraine and Linda. Edinburgh: Inner Keltia.

Napier, A. David. 1986. *Masks, Transformation and Paradox*. London: Thames and Hudson.

Nash-Williams, V. E. 1950. *The Early Christian Monuments of Wales*. Cardiff: University of Wales Press.

Newark, Tim. 1988. *Celtic Warriors 400 BC–AD 1600*. London: Blandford.

Nichols, J. 1828. *The Progresses, Processions, and Magnificent Festivities, of King James the First, His Royal Consort, Family, and Court*. London: Nichols.

Nichols, Ross. 1990. *The Book of Druidry*. London: Aquarian.

Nicoll, Allardyce. 1931. *Masks, Mimes and Miracles: Studies in the Popular Theatre*. London: Harrap.

Nilsson, Martin P. 1920. *Primitive Time-reckoning*. Lund: Gleerup.

North, C. N. McIntyre. 1881. *Leabhar Comunn nam Fior Ghael—The Book of the Club of True Highlanders: A Record of the Press, Arms, Customs, Arts and Science of the Highlanders*. 2 vols. London: Smythson.

O'Begly, Conor, and Hugh MacCurtain. 1732. *The English Irish Dictionary*. Paris: Guérin.

O'Boyle, Sean. 1980. *Ogham: The Poet's Secret*. Dublin: Dalton.

Ó Cuiv, Brian. 1980. "Irish Worlds for 'Alphabet.'" *Ériu* 31: 100–110.

O'Curry, Eugene. 1873. *On the Manners and Customs of the Ancient Irish*. 3 vols. London: Williams and Norgate.

O'Connell, John. 1916. *The Honan Hostel Chapel Cork*. Cork: Guy and Co.

O'Donovan, John. 1842. *The Banquet of Dun Na-gedh and the Battle of Magh Rath: An Ancient Historical Tale*. Dublin: Irish Archeological Society.

———. 1845. *A Grammar of the Irish Language*. Dublin: Hodges and Smith.

———, ed. 1847. *Leabhar na g-Ceart, or the Book of Rights*. Dublin: Celtic Society.

———, ed. 1856. *Annals of the Kingdom of Ireland, by the Four Masters*. Dublin: Hodges, Smith, and Co.

———, trans. 1868. *Sanas Chormaic—Cormac's Glossary*. Edited and annotated by Whitley Stokes. Calcutta: Irish Archæological and Celtic Society.

O'Flaherty, Roderic. 1793. *Ogygia, or, a Chronological Account of Irish Events*. Translated by James Hely. 2 vols. Dublin: M'Kenzie. [Original Latin edition: *Ogygia, seu, rerum Hibernicarum chronologia*. London, 1685.]

O'Grady, Standish H., ed. and trans. 1892. *Silva Gadelica (I–XXXI): A Collection of Tales in Irish*. London: Williams and Norgate.

O'Hehir, Brendan. 1989. "The Origin, Development and History of the Ogham Script: Facts and Conjecture." In *Exploring Rock Art*, edited by Donald L. Cyr. Santa Barbara: Stonehenge Viewpoint.

Ó hÓgáin, Dáithi. 1981. *Myth, Legend and Romance: An Encyclopedia of the Irish Folk Tradition*. London: Ryan.

O'Keefe, J. G., ed. and trans. 1913. *Buile Suibhne (The frenzy of Suibhne) Being the Adventures of Subhne Geilt, a Middle Irish Romance*. London: Irish Texts Society.

O'Kelleher, A., and G. Schoepperle, ed. and trans. 1918. *Betha Collum Chille— Life of Columcille*. Urbana: University of Illinois.

O'Murnaghan, Art. 1924–1951. *Leabhar na hAiséirighe (The Book of Resurrection)*. Dublin: National Museum of Ireland.

O'Rahilly, T. F. 1946. *Early Irish History and Mythology*. Dublin: Institute For Advanced Studies.

Ó Tuathaigh, Gearóid. 1972. *Ireland Before the Famine, 1798–1848*. Dublin: Gill and Macmillan.

Oufle, Caspar. 1830. "Demonology and Witchcraft." *The National Magazine* 1.5 (Nov.): 585–98.

Owen, Trefor M. 1959. *Welsh Folk Customs*. Cardiff: Lewis and Sons.

———. 2016. *The Customs and Traditions of Wales: A Pocket Guide*. Revised by Emma Lile. Cardiff: University of Wales Press.

Painter, K. S. 1977. *The Mildenhall Treasure*. London: British Museum.

Palmer, Roy. 1992. *The Folklore of Hereford and Worcester*. Woonton Almeley: Logaston.

Patch, Howard Rollin. 1950. *The Other World According to Descriptions in Medieval Literature*. Cambridge, MA: Harvard University Press.

Pegg, Bob. 1981. *Rites and Riots: Folk Customs of Britain and Europe*. London: Blandford.

Pennar, Meirion, trans. 1989. *The Black Book of Carmarthen*. Lampeter: Llanerch.

Pennick, Nigel. 1978. *Ogham and Runic: Magical Writing of Old Britain and Northern Europe*. Bar Hill: Fenris-Wolf.

———. 1988. *Games of the Gods*. London: Rider.

————. 1990. "The Origin of Ogam and Runestaves." In *Celtic Secrets*, edited by Donald L. Cyr. Santa Barbara: Stonehenge Viewpoint.

————. 1992. *Celtic Art in the Northern Tradition*. Bar Hill: Nideck.

————. 1993. *Anima Loci*. Bar Hill: Nideck.

————. 1994. *Practical Magic in the Northern Tradition*. Loughborough: Thoth.

————. 1995. *Secrets of East Anglian Magic*. London: Hale.

————. 1996a. *Celtic Sacred Landscapes*. London: Thames and Hudson.

————. 1996b. *Secret Signs, Symbols and Sigils*. Chieveley: Capall Bann.

————. 1997a. *The Celtic Cross*. London: Blandford.

————. 1997b. *The Celtic Saints*. London: Thorsons.

————. 1997c. *The Sacred World of the Celts*. London: Thorsons.

————. 1998. *Crossing the Borderlines. Guising, Masking and Ritual Animal Disguises in the European Tradition*. Chieveley: Capall Bann.

————, ed. 1999a. *Plenydd: The Welsh Bardic Alphabet*. Bar Hill: Library of the European Tradition.

————. 1999b. *The Complete Illustrated Guide to Runes*. Shaftesbury: Element.

Pennick, Nigel, and Helen Field. 1996. *The Goddess Year*. Chieveley: Capall Bann.

————. 1998. *The God Year*. Chieveley: Capall Bann.

Pennick, Nigel, and Nigel Jackson. 1992. *The Celtic Oracle: The Ancient Art of the Druids*. London: Aquarian/Thorsons.

Peter, Thurstan. 1997 [1912]. *The Cornish Obby Oss*. Penzance: Oakmagic.

Pittaway, Andy, and Bernard Scofield. 1976. *The Complete Country Bizarre*. London: Astragal.

Planck, Dieter, and Jörg Biel et al., eds. 1985. *Der Keltenfürst von Hochdorf, Methoden und Ergebnisse der Landesarchäologie*. Stuttgart: Thiess.

Pokorny, Julius. 1953. *Keltologie*. Bern: Francke.

Portal, Frédéric. 1938. *Des couleurs symboliques dans l'Antiquité, le Moyen-Age et les temps modernes*. Paris: Niclaus.

Porteous, Alexander. 1928. *Forest Folklore*. London: Allen and Unwin.

Pughe, John, trans. 1865. *The Physicians of Myddvai: Maddygon Myddfai, or the Medical Practice of the Celebrated Rhiwallon and His Sons, of Myddvai, in Carmarthenshire, Physicians to Rhys Gryg, Lord of Dynevor and Ystrad Towy, About the Middle of the Thirteenth Century*. Edited by John Williams Ab Ithel. Llandovery: Welsh Manuscripts Society.

Raglan, Lady. 1939. "The 'Green Man' in Church Architecture." *Folklore* 50.1 (March): 45–57.

Redknap, Mark. 1991. *The Christian Celts: Treasure of Late Celtic Wales*. Cardiff: National Museum of Wales.

Rees, Alwyn, and Brinley Rees. 1967. *Celtic Heritage*. London: Thames and Hudson.

Reuter, Otto Sigfrid. 1934. *Germanische Himmelskunde*. Munich: Lehmann.

Rhys, Ernest, ed. 1912. *The Itinerary Through Wales and the Description of Wales by Giraldus Cambrensis*. London: Dent.

Rhŷs, John. 1901. *Celtic Folklore*. 2 vols. Oxford: Oxford University Press.

Rich, Barnaby. 1610. *A New Description of Ireland*. London: Adams.

Richardson, L. J. D. 1943. "The Word 'Ogham.'" *Hermathena* 62: 96–105.

Ross, Anne. 1967. *Pagan Celtic Britain*. London: Cardinal.

———. 1976. *The Folklore of the Scottish Highlands*. London: Batsford.

———. 1986a. *Druids, Gods and Heroes of Celtic Mythology*. London: Routledge and Kegan Paul.

———. 1986b. *The Pagan Celts*. London: Batsford.

Scott, Michael. 1983. *Irish Folk and Fairy Tales*. 2 vols. London: Sphere.

Seignolle, Claude. 1963. *Le Folklore de la Provence*. Paris: Maisonneuve et larose.

Sharkey, John, ed. 1992. *Ogham Monuments in Wales*. Texts by R. Rolt Brash and J. Romilly Allen. Llanerch: Felinfach.

Sharp, William. 1920. *The Winged Destiny: Studies in the Spiritual History of the Gael by "Fiona Macleod."* London: Heinemann.

Shaw, William. 1780. *Galic and English Dictionary: All the Words in the Scotch and Irish Dialects of the Celtic that Could Be Collected from the Voice, and Old Books and Manuscripts*. 2 vols. London: Murray.

Sheehy, Jeanne. 1980. *The Rediscovery of Ireland's Past: The Celtic Revival, 1830–1930*. London: Thames and Hudson.

Skene, William F., trans. 1868. *The Four Ancient Books of Wales Containing the Cymric Poems Attributed to the Bards of the Sixth Century*. 2 vols. Edinburgh: Edmonston and Douglas.

Sills-Fuchs, Martha. 1990. *Der Mittagshirsch: Die Wiederentdeckung des keltischen Kalenders*. Vienna: Edition S.

Simpson, Jacqueline. 1987. *European Mythology*. London: Hamlyn.

Sjoestedt, Marie-Louise. 1982. *Gods and Heroes of the Celts*. Berkeley: University of California Press.

Spence, Lewis. 1928. *The Mysteries of Britain*. London: Rider.

———. 1970. *The Magic Arts in Celtic Britain*. London: Aquarian.

Stewart, R. J. 1986. *The Prophetic Vision of Merlin*. London: Arkana.

Stokes, Whitney, ed. and trans. 1895. "The Prose Tales in the Rennes *Dindshenchas.*" *Revue Celtique* 16: 31–83, 135–67, 269–312.

———, ed. and trans. 1900. "Da Choca's Hostel." *Revue Celtique* 21: 149–65, 312–27, 388–402.

———, ed. and trans. 1905. "The Colloquy of the Two Sages, *Immacallam in dá Thuarad.*" *Revue Celtique* 26: 4–64.

Strutt, Joseph. 1830. *The Sports and Pastimes of the People of England.* Edited by William Hone. London: Reaves.

Suggett, Richard. 2006–2007. "Poets and Carpenters: Creating the Architecture of Happiness in Late-Medieval Wales." *Proceedings of the Harvard Celtic Colloquium* 26/27: 241–68.

Tabor, Raymond. 1994. *Traditional Woodland Crafts.* London: Batsford.

Tiddy, R. J. E. 1923. *The Mummers' Play.* Oxford: Clarendon.

Thurneysen, Rudolf. 1921. *Die irische Heiden- und Königssage.* Haale/Saale: Niemeyer.

Tolkien, J. R. R. 1964. *Tree and Leaf.* London: Allen and Unwin.

Toynbee, J. M. C. 1962. *Art in Roman Britain.* London: Thames and Hudson.

Varagnac, André. 1948. *Civilisation traditionelle et genres de vie.* Paris: Michel.

Vendryes, Joseph. 1941–1948. "L'écriture ogamique et ses origines." *Études Celtiques* 4.1: 83–116.

Wade-Evans, A. W. 1944. *Vitae Sanctorum Britanniae et Genealogiae.* Cardiff: University of Wales Press.

Waterhouse, George. 1852. *Ornamental Irish Antiquities* [brochure]. Dublin: Waterhouse.

Webster, G. 1986. *The British Celts and their Gods Under Rome.* London: Batsford.

White, G. Pawley (Gunwyn). 1972. *A Handbook of Cornish Surnames.* Camborne: privately published.

Wickham, Glynne. 1966. *Early English Stages 1300 to 1660.* Vol. I: *1300 to 1576.* London: Routledge and Kegan Paul.

Wilde, Lady. 1902. *Ancient Legends, Mystic Charms and Superstitions of Ireland.* New edition. London: Chatto and Windus.

Williams, G. J. 1956. *Iolo Morganwg.* Cardiff: University of Wales Press.

———. 1957. "Glamorgan Customs in the 18th Century." *Gwerin* 1.3: 99–108.

———. 1954–1955. "William Robert o'r Ydwal." *Llan Cymru* 3: 48–50.

Williams, G. J., and Evan J. Jones, eds. 1934. *Gramadegau'r penceirddiaid.* Cardiff: University of Wales Press.

Williams, Ifor, and Thomas Roberts, eds. 1914. *Cywyddau Dafydd ap Gwilym a'i Gyfoeswr.* Bangor: Thomas.

Williams, Ifor, and J. Llywelyn Williams, eds. 1939. *Gwaith Guto'r Glyn.* Cardiff: University of Wales Press.

Williams Ab Ithel, John, trans. 1856. *Dosparth Edeyrn Davod Aur; or, The Ancient Welsh Grammar.* Llandovery and London: Rees/Longman and Co.

———, ed. 1862–1874. *Barddas; or, a Collection of Original Documents, Illustrative of the Theology, Wisdom, and Usages of the Bardo-Druidic System of the Isle of Britain.* 2 vols. Llandovery and London: Roderic/Quaritch.

Wilson, Steve. 1993. *Robin Hood: The Spirit of the Forest.* London: Neptune.

Wimberley, L. C. 1928. *Folklore of the English and Scottish Ballads.* New York: Unger.

Woll, Johanna. 1991. *Alte Festbrauche im Jahreslauf.* Stuttgart: Ulmer.

Wood-Martin, W. G. 1895. *Pagan Ireland.* London: Longmans, Green, and Co.

———, 1902. *Traces of the Elder Faiths of Ireland.* London: Longmans, Green, and Co.

Woods, K. S. 1949. *Rural Crafts of England.* London: Harrap.

Wright, Dudley. 1924. *Druidism: The Ancient Faith of Britain.* London and Cheltenham: Burrow.

Wright, Philip A. 1974. *Old Farm Implements.* Newton Abbot: David and Charles.

York, Michael. 1995. *The Divine versus the Asurian: An Interpretation of Indo-European Cult and Myth.* Bethesda, MD: International Scholars.

Index

Page references in *italics* refer to illustrations.

Bardo-Druidic spirituality, v, 141–42.
See also Celtic spirituality
cosmic axis, 79, 114
Bards, 29, 83–85, 115, 134–37,
146. See also under names of
individual Bards
Baring-Gould, S., 112
Bar Ogham, 68
Barrett, Francis, 120–22
Battle Ogham, 62–63
Beith, 30–37
aicme of, 143
Bell Trees, 85
Bendigeidfran, 131–32
besoms, 103–8
jumping the broomstick, 107
time for making, 104
and witches, 105
bile, 76, 85
Bilwg, Ieuan du'r, 129–30
Birch, 30–31, 78
Celtic lore of, 100–108
primacy in the Oghams, 9–11
and sexuality, 107–8
Blackthorn, 51
Black Wood, 82
Blake, William, xvi, 29
Blegywryd, 131
Bog Oaks, 42
Book of Ballymote, The, xii, 23
described, 15–16
Ogham in, 15–19
Boru, Brian, 83
Bourdichon, Jean, 114
Bourtree, 53
Brampton Oak, 114
Bran, King, 35–36
Brehon Laws, 14

Breugel, Peter, 91
Briatharogaim, xiii
Brocéliande, 80
Broom, 54–55
Broom-Cow, 103
broomsticks, 103. See also besoms
Buain, Bailé Mac, 14–15

"Cad Goddeu," 39, 54, 60
Caerwys Tree, 86
Caesar, Julius, 82
Caledon, Wood of, 80–82
Callirius Silvanus, 73
Cambrensis, Giraldus, 47
Ceart Ogam, 28
Celtic cross, 106
Celtic Oracle, The (deck), 21
Celtic Revival, 6, 117, 127
Celtic spirituality, 142
art in, 84
Celtic spiritual landscape, viii
cosmic axis, 79, 114
creation myth, 123–24
eternal flow of waters–cyclic nature
of events, 116
sacred symbolism in, 132
transmitted from mouth to ear,
115
veneration of trees, 73–75
Celtic Tree Alphabets. See also aibítir;
Coelbren alphabet; Ogham
ancient and modern manifestations,
xi–xvi
Ogham as, 23
Celtic Tree Oracle, The (deck), 21
cerddorion, 146
Charles II, King, 92–93
Charms of the Bards, 134